USBORNE
INTERNET-LINKED
GREEKS

Susan Peach
and Anne Millard

Illustrated by Ian Jackson

Edited by Jane Chisholm and Eileen O'Brien
History consultant: Graham Tingay

Cover design by Neil Francis

Designed by Robert Walster, Radhi Parekh, Iain Ashman and Sar___

Additional illustrations by Richard Draper, Robert Walster, Gerry Wood, Peter Dennis, Nigel Wright and Gillian Hurry

With thanks to Anthony Marks, Abigail Wheatley and Georgina Andrews

Cover photo credits: Main: Neil Francis, with special thanks to Arms and Archery
Background: © Araldo de Luca/Corbis

Contents

How to use this book

Dates

Many dates in this book are from the time before the birth of Christ. They are shown by the letters BC, which stand for 'Before Christ'. Dates in the period after Christ's birth are shown by AD, which stand for *Anno Domini*, or 'Year of our Lord'.

Dates in the BC period are counted backwards from the birth of Christ. The main centuries are:

```
1-99BC      = first century BC
100-199BC  = second century BC
200-299BC  = third century BC
300-399BC  = fourth century BC
400-499BC  = fifth century BC
500-599BC  = sixth century BC
600-699BC  = seventh century BC
```

Some dates begin with 'c.'. This stands for *circa*, the Latin word for 'about'. It is used when experts aren't sure exactly when something happened.

Periods of Greek history

Experts divide ancient Greek history into several approximate periods, which are shown below. These have been used throughout the book.

```
c.2900-1000BC = The Bronze Age
c.1100-800BC  = The Dark Ages
c.800-500BC   = The Archaic Period
c.500-336BC   = The Classical Period
c.336-30BC    = The Hellenistic Period
```

How we know about the Greeks

Although the ancient Greeks lived about three thousand years ago, we know a lot about how they lived. Our information comes from many different sources, some of which are shown here.

Archaeologists have dug up many ancient Greek objects and buildings. Important sites have been excavated in Greece and in the places that the Greeks colonized. Underwater archaeologists have found the wrecks of several ancient Greek ships, some with their cargoes preserved. Greek objects have also been found in countries where they were taken by traders. For example, Minoan pots made on Crete have been discovered in ancient Egyptian tombs (see page 5).

Archaeologists at work on a site

Pots are some of the most useful archaeological finds. The Greeks decorated many of their pots with pictures

of everyday life. These scenes have given experts a lot of information about the Greeks. Many scenes in this book are based on pictures found on vases.

This vase shows potters at work.

When the Romans captured Greece in the second century BC, they were fascinated by the buildings, statues and paintings they found.

They were so impressed by Greek art that they made copies of many statues and paintings. A large number of these Roman copies have survived, although the originals have been lost.

This discus thrower is a Roman copy of a Greek statue. The Greek original has been lost.

The Greeks wrote on scrolls made out of a plant called papyrus. This rots easily, so very few original manuscripts have been found. But Greek writings have survived because people from Roman times onward made copies of them. The copies include works by many Greek writers about history, philosophy and politics, as well as plays and poems. Coins, clay tablets and inscriptions on monuments and buildings provide other written evidence.

Part of an inscription from the wall of a Greek temple

Silver coin from Athens

Fragment of Greek papyrus found in Egypt

Key dates

On some pages of this book there are charts that list the events of the particular period. There's also a chart on pages 88-89 that lists all the events mentioned in the book.

Unfamiliar words

Some words in the ancient Greek language are written in *italic* type. These words, and some other words, are explained in the glossary on pages 90-91. You can also read more about some of the people in this book by looking up their names in the 'Who was who' section, on pages 85-87.

Places

Maps on many pages of this book show where events took place. Towns or cities are marked with dots, and battles are shown with crosses. The area now known as Turkey is marked as Asia Minor, which was its name in ancient times.

Internet links

If you have access to a computer with an Internet connection, you can try out the websites described in this book. For links to these sites, go to **www.usborne-quicklinks.com** For more information, see the inside front cover.

The first Greeks

Map of Greece

GREECE
AEGEAN SEA
MEDITERRANEAN SEA
CYCLADES ISLANDS
CRETE

Greece is in southern Europe. The mainland is surrounded by many Greek islands in the Mediterranean Sea.

The first people arrived in Greece around 40,000 years ago. They lived in caves, hunting and gathering food. Some time before 6000BC, farming was introduced by new peoples from the east, who settled in eastern Greece.

The first farmers grew vegetables and grain, and kept sheep.

Around 3000BC, people in Greece learned how to mix copper and tin to make bronze. Bronze tools were harder and sharper than those made of bone or flint. This made farming and building easier. The time from 3000-1100BC is known as the Bronze Age. These objects were made at this time.

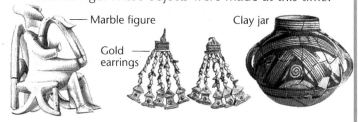

Marble figure

Gold earrings

Clay jar

As farming became more efficient, many farmers exchanged their surplus produce for other goods. Some people stopped farming, and crafted goods to sell. Trade made people more prosperous, the population increased and villages grew into towns.

Farm produce could be exchanged for goods such as tools or pottery.

From 2600-2000BC the people of the Cyclades islands were very prosperous. There was a lot of trade between the islands. But the Cyclades were too small to develop further and it was on Crete that the first great European civilization began.

Crete

Early Crete

CRETE
Knossos
Mallia
Zakro
Hagia Triada
Phaestos

The first inhabitants of Crete were probably farmers, who settled there around 6000BC. By around 2000BC there was a flourishing civilization on the island, with a highly organized economy and system of trade, based around a number of large palaces. There were skilled craft workers and artists, and some people could read and write. Here are some objects made by Cretan craftsmen.

Gold ornament

Statue of a bull

Rock crystal vase

We know about this early civilization from archaeological evidence found on Crete. In AD1894, an archaeologist named Arthur Evans began excavating a palace at Knossos (see map above). Evans named the civilization Minoan, after a legendary Cretan king named Minos.

The legend of Minos

According to legend, the god Zeus (see page 64) fell in love with a beautiful princess named Europa. He changed himself into a bull and swam to Crete with her on his back. She had three sons, Minos, Sarpedon and Rhadamanthys. Minos became the king of Crete, and his palace was at Knossos.

Although the legend says that Minos was the name of one king, experts think that Minos may have been a title, like the Egyptian word Pharaoh. All Cretan kings may have been known as Minos.

Life in Minoan Crete

An extra piece of cloth could be worn like an apron.

Short kilt

Flounced skirt

A belt of twisted cloth was tied around the waist.

We know what the Minoans wore because their clothes were shown in many wall paintings. Men usually wore a loincloth and a short kilt of wool or linen.

Women wore bright, elaborate dresses, usually with tight bodices which left their breasts bare. The skirts were generally flounced.

Most people made their living from farming. They kept animals and grew crops such as wheat, barley, olives and grapes. Fishing and hunting provided extra food. This wall painting shows a fisherman.

Areas where Minoans traded

MAINLAND GREECE

ASIA MINOR

Knossos

CYCLADES

CRETE

EGYPT

Map of Minoan trade

The Minoans made frequent journeys abroad, as well as on Crete itself. They used carts, but there were few roads, so sea travel was popular.

The Greek historian Thucydides says that King Minos had a large fleet of ships, which controlled the seas. The wall painting above shows several Minoan ships.

The Minoans traded with many foreign countries. Their pots and other goods have been found in Greece and the Cyclades, and all around the Mediterranean area.

Writing

When the Minoans started to store and export goods, they developed a system of writing to help them keep accurate records. Their first script, which was used c.2000BC, was a form of hieroglyphic (picture) writing. In around 1900BC they introduced a second script, which we call Linear A. As yet, no one has been able to decipher either of these scripts.

Part of a Linear A tablet

This disc, from Phaestos, is inscribed with a third Minoan script, which has not yet been deciphered.

Pottery

Minoan pots

Before the discovery of Knossos, Minoan pots had been found in Egypt. These pots had already been approximately dated, as experts had been able to establish dates for Egyptian sites. When a style of pot was found on Crete, archaeologists could date it by comparing it with the pots found in Egypt. This also meant that they could give a rough date to the Cretan site where the pot had been found.

The Minoan palaces

The Minoans often built towns by the coast, where they could easily reach the sea and fertile farmlands. Larger towns were based around a palace. The first palaces, built soon after 2000BC, were destroyed by earthquakes around 300 years later.

Little remains of these buildings, because the Minoans built new, even grander palaces over them. Four of these later palaces have been found, at Knossos, Zakro, Phaestos and Mallia. There's also a large villa at Hagia Triada and a few smaller sites.

The palace at Knossos

The largest palace, at Knossos, was rebuilt several times between around 1900BC and 1450BC. This picture shows how it probably looked at its largest. It covered around 20,000m square (215,000ft square), and experts think that over 30,000 people lived in the palace and surrounding area.

The palace was decorated with images of bulls' horns.

The roofs, ceilings and doors were made of wood.

Water and drainage

Knossos had an excellent water supply and drainage system. To prevent floods, gutters were built to channel spring and autumn rains. The water was stored in tanks and passed into the palace along clay pipes. The system served several toilets and bathrooms. This picture shows a royal bathroom.

Decoration

Each palace had some particularly luxurious apartments. They may have been designed for the royal family. They had large, airy rooms, decorated with wall paintings known as frescoes. These were made by applying paint to wet plaster. The frescoes at Knossos have given archaeologists a lot of valuable information about Minoan dress and customs. Most of the frescoes which can now be seen in the palace are modern reconstructions, based on fragments of the original pictures.

This fresco shows a young man wearing an elaborate headdress. This suggests that he was a prince or a king.

Many paintings depict the beauty of nature. This fresco shows dolphins and other fish.

Lighting

Light was let into the building through open shafts which ran from the roof to the ground floor. These are known as light wells. Staircases and corridors led from the light wells to the rooms on each level.

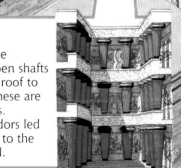

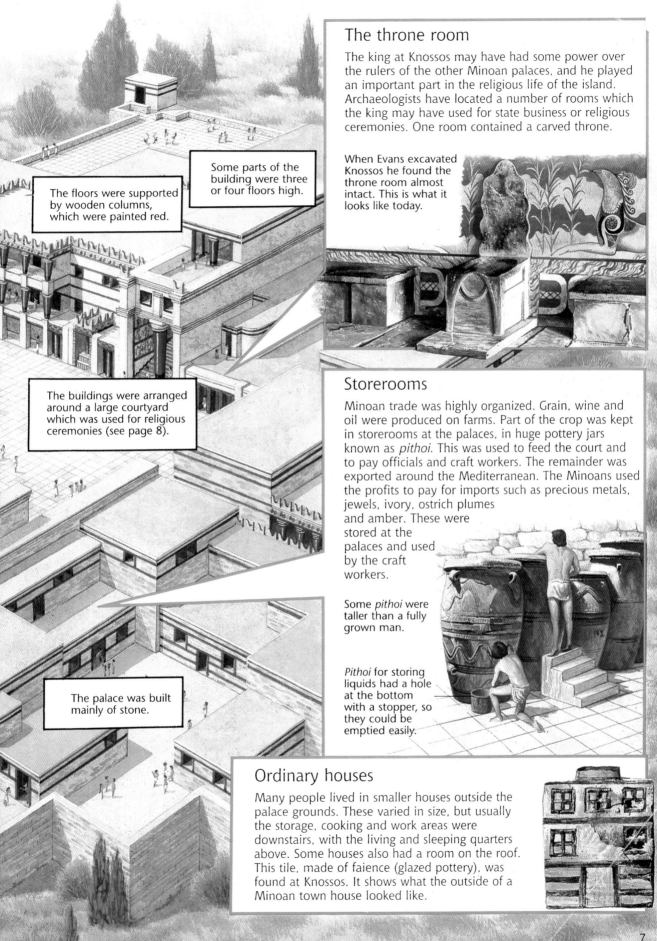

The throne room

The king at Knossos may have had some power over the rulers of the other Minoan palaces, and he played an important part in the religious life of the island. Archaeologists have located a number of rooms which the king may have used for state business or religious ceremonies. One room contained a carved throne.

When Evans excavated Knossos he found the throne room almost intact. This is what it looks like today.

Some parts of the building were three or four floors high.

The floors were supported by wooden columns, which were painted red.

The buildings were arranged around a large courtyard which was used for religious ceremonies (see page 8).

The palace was built mainly of stone.

Storerooms

Minoan trade was highly organized. Grain, wine and oil were produced on farms. Part of the crop was kept in storerooms at the palaces, in huge pottery jars known as *pithoi*. This was used to feed the court and to pay officials and craft workers. The remainder was exported around the Mediterranean. The Minoans used the profits to pay for imports such as precious metals, jewels, ivory, ostrich plumes and amber. These were stored at the palaces and used by the craft workers.

Some *pithoi* were taller than a fully grown man.

Pithoi for storing liquids had a hole at the bottom with a stopper, so they could be emptied easily.

Ordinary houses

Many people lived in smaller houses outside the palace grounds. These varied in size, but usually the storage, cooking and work areas were downstairs, with the living and sleeping quarters above. Some houses also had a room on the roof. This tile, made of faience (glazed pottery), was found at Knossos. It shows what the outside of a Minoan town house looked like.

Minoan religion

For a link to a website where you can find out more about the Minoan religion, go to **www.usborne-quicklinks.com**

Archaeological remains have shown that special rooms were set aside for religious ceremonies in Minoan palaces. Outdoor shrines were also used.

It seems that goddesses were more important than gods, as they are shown more often in statues and paintings. Some of them are shown below.

The goddess on this seal is known as the Mistress of the Animals. She is shown surrounded by animals.

This seal shows a goddess who looked after crops. She is often shown by a sacred tree, sometimes with a young god.

This goddess protected the household. She is often depicted with snakes, which were a sacred symbol.

Sacred symbols

The Minoans had two sacred symbols which they used to decorate palaces, tombs and pots. The bull was thought to be sacred and images of its horns were found throughout Knossos. Another common symbol was a weapon, known as the *labrys*.

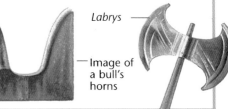

Labrys

Image of a bull's horns

Religious ceremonies

This reconstruction shows what might have happened at a religious ceremony. Special priests and priestesses would have led the ceremony. Archaeological remains show that food, statues and weapons were offered to the gods.

A *libation* (an offering of milk, wine or blood) was poured on to an altar.

Musicians

Sacred symbols and statues of gods

Altar

Offerings

Bull-leaping

This fresco shows part of the bull-leaping ritual. The figure on the right was there to catch the leaper.

One of the strangest Minoan practices was bull-leaping. Teams of men and women approached a charging bull and one by one they grasped its horns, leaped on to its back, and then to the ground. Experts believe this was a religious ritual, as the bull was a sacred animal. The ceremony may have taken place in the palace courtyard.

Death and the afterlife

The Minoans believed in life after death. They buried people with food and personal possessions which they thought would be of use in the afterlife. Early tombs, from around 2800BC, were round stone structures which were used for many burials. Later, the Minoans used individual coffins.

This coffin, found at the villa of Hagia Triada, was made in about 1400BC. It is decorated with a funeral scene, showing people making offerings.

The end of the Minoans

All the palaces on Crete were destroyed around 1450BC. Experts link this to a volcanic eruption on Thera, an island which lies to the north of Crete. The explosions were so violent that most of Thera was blasted away, leaving only the small island now called Santorini. On Crete, this may have caused tidal waves, earth tremors and flooding. But recent geological evidence has cast doubt on the dating of the eruption, so Minoan dates may have to be revised when more evidence is found.

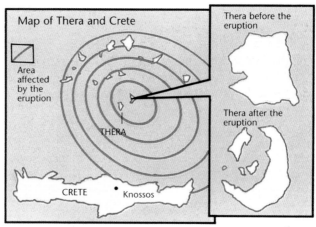

Map of Thera and Crete

Area affected by the eruption

THERA

CRETE   • Knossos

Thera before the eruption

Thera after the eruption

The arrival of the Mycenaeans

Natural disasters may not have been the only cause of the Minoans' downfall. According to legend, King Minos went to Sicily, where he was killed by a local king and his fleet was destroyed. This may be partly true. Perhaps there was an expedition which resulted in the loss of Crete's fleet. We do know that by around 1450BC, Crete was invaded by a people from mainland Greece, known as the Mycenaeans.

The Mycenaeans rebuilt the palace at Knossos and became the new rulers of the island.

Around 1400BC the palace at Knossos burned down and was abandoned.

Around 50 years later Knossos was destroyed again. We do not know why this happened. Perhaps the Mycenaeans fought among themselves, or new conquerors arrived from mainland Greece. Another theory is that the Minoans rebelled against the Mycenaeans. Between 1400BC and 1100BC a joint Minoan-Mycenaean culture flourished, but Crete was no longer a powerful nation. By 1100BC, Minoan culture had collapsed.

The Minotaur

According to a later Greek legend, an Athenian prince named Theseus went to Crete, where he fought and killed a terrible monster known as the Minotaur. It was half man, half bull and was kept in a maze known as the Labyrinth. You can read the full story of Theseus on page 82.

Perhaps there was some truth in this legend. The palace at Knossos had so many rooms and corridors, it might have seemed like a maze. It may have been known as the *Labyrinth*, or house of the *labrys*, because it was decorated with many images of the sacred weapon.

The Minotaur could also have been based on fact. It's possible that the king wore the mask of a bull's head during religious rituals. People may gradually have forgotten about the king and begun to believe in a monster.

Key dates

c.6000BC The first farmers arrive on Crete and the Greek mainland.

c.3000BC People in Greece discover how to make bronze. Start of the Bronze Age.

c.2000BC The first palaces are built on Crete.

c.1900BC The Minoans start to use the Linear A script.

c.1700BC The first palaces are destroyed by earthquake. New palaces are built.

c.1600BC The first Mycenaeans arrive on Crete.

c.1450BC Traditional date for the destruction of Thera. Recent evidence suggests that this date may have to be revised (see above).

c.1400BC Final destruction of the palace at Knossos.

c.1100BC End of Minoan culture.

The Mycenaeans

From around 1600-1100BC, mainland Greece was dominated by a people known as the Mycenaeans, who lived in small kingdoms. Their name comes from the city of Mycenae, where remains of their culture were first discovered. Some experts believe that the Mycenaeans invaded Greece from central Europe. Others think that they had been in Greece for some time, and only gradually became the dominant people. They were never politically united, but the Mycenaeans were linked by their culture. They all spoke an early form of the Greek language and shared a common way of life.

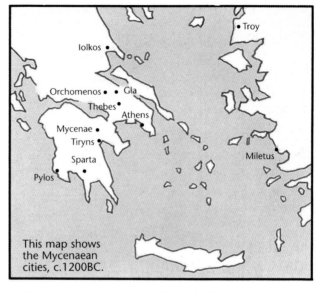

This map shows the Mycenaean cities, c.1200BC.

The royal graves

Some of the first and most important archaeological evidence about the Mycenaeans comes from the royal graves at Mycenae, which date from 1600BC. There were two main styles of graves: shaft graves and *tholos* tombs.

Shaft graves

The earliest tombs were shaft graves, like the one shown in this cutaway reconstruction. Shaft graves could be over 12m (40ft) deep and usually contained several bodies, perhaps from the same family.

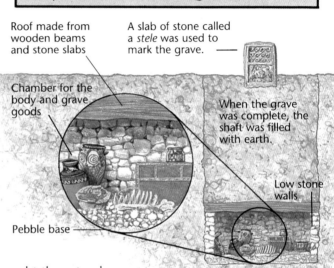

Roof made from wooden beams and stone slabs

A slab of stone called a *stele* was used to mark the grave.

Chamber for the body and grave goods

When the grave was complete, the shaft was filled with earth.

Low stone walls

Pebble base

Tholos tombs

By around 1500BC, shaft graves had been replaced by the *tholos*, or beehive-shaped tomb. The reconstruction below shows one which dates from c.1250BC, from the city of Mycenae.

It was once thought these tombs were treasure stores, because of their rich grave goods. This *tholos* is still called the Treasury of Atreus, after a legendary king. You can read all about Atreus on page 83.

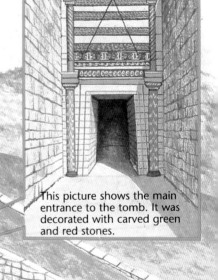

This picture shows the main entrance to the tomb. It was decorated with carved green and red stones.

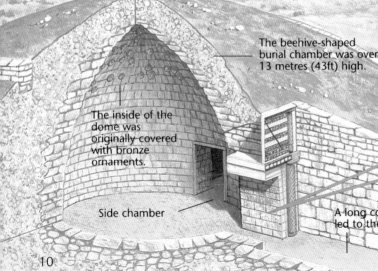

The beehive-shaped burial chamber was over 13 metres (43ft) high.

The inside of the dome was originally covered with bronze ornaments.

Side chamber

A long corridor called a *dromos* led to the entrance.

For a link to a website with an interactive map of the Mycenaean royal tombs, go to **www.usborne-quicklinks.com**

Tomb treasures

Members of the royal families were buried with precious objects. Shaft graves were difficult for tomb robbers to break into, and so have often survived with their goods intact. The objects shown here were found in graves at Mycenae.

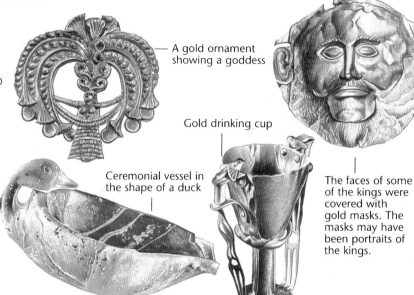

A gold ornament showing a goddess

Gold drinking cup

Ceremonial vessel in the shape of a duck

The faces of some of the kings were covered with gold masks. The masks may have been portraits of the kings.

Sword and dagger blades were bronze, but the hilts were often made of gold.

Religion

Wall paintings, statues and shrines show that the Mycenaeans had similar beliefs to the Minoans. The Mycenaeans did not build temples, but rooms were set aside for worship in houses and palaces.

Outdoor shrines were also set up.

Their elaborate tombs show that they believed in a life after death. They thought that goods from this world would be of use in the afterlife and would help wealthy people to preserve the privileges they had on Earth.

Outdoor shrines, like the one shown on this gold ornament, were built in the countryside.

As in Crete, goddesses seem to have been the most powerful deities. Mycenaean records mention several gods and goddesses, such as Zeus, Poseidon and Dionysus, who were to be important in later Greek history.

The figure on this fresco, shown holding ears of corn, may be an early version of the goddess Demeter (see page 65).

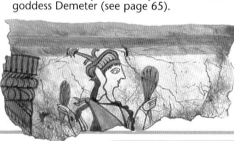

This terracotta figurine represents a Mycenaean goddess.

Clothes

Statuettes and frescoes give us an idea of what fashions were like in Mycenaean days. They seem to have resembled fashions in Crete. The fresco below shows a court lady.

Young men, like the ones shown out hunting, on the dagger blade above, seem to have been clean shaven. Many of the gold masks from shaft graves show bearded men, but this may have been an older man's style.

Key dates

c.2000BC First evidence of the Mycenaeans in Greece.

c.1650-1550BC Grave circle A is in use at Mycenae (see page 12).

c.1600BC The height of Mycenaean power, economy and culture.

c.1450BC The Mycenaeans occupy the palace of Knossos on Crete and become the rulers of the island.

c.1250BC Defensive walls are built around many Mycenaean cities. Traditional date of the fall of Troy.

c.1200BC Start of the period of Mycenaean decline. Their cities are gradually abandoned.

c.1100BC Start of the Dark Ages.

Mycenaean cities

Each Mycenaean kingdom had its own city. Cities were usually built on high ground and were enclosed by defensive walls. This type of fortified city is called an *acropolis*, which means 'high city'.

An *acropolis* contained a palace along with houses for courtiers, soldiers and craftsmen. It was also a military and administrative headquarters and a workplace for many craft workers.

The acropolis at Mycenae

The earliest Mycenaean cities were often destroyed when new ones were built on the same sites. The buildings in this view of the ruins at Mycenae date from the end of the Mycenaean period.

The Lion Gate

Two lion sculptures decorated the main gateway. These may have been the symbols of the royal family. Around 1250BC, huge walls were built around the *acropolis*. In some parts they were 7m (23ft) thick.

Grave circle A

A burial ground for the royal family, now known as grave circle A, was situated just inside the city walls. It consisted of a number of shaft graves, enclosed by a circular stone wall.

City walls
The Lion Gate
Grave circle A
Houses

Writing

Clay tablets covered with writing have been found in some Mycenaean cities. The Mycenaeans learned the art of writing from the Minoans. They combined some signs from Linear A with new signs, to produce a script to suit their language. This script is known as Linear B, and it has been deciphered. The tablets give a good idea of life in the palaces, as they list many goods and job titles.

Mycenaean scribes at work

An example of Linear B script

Trade

The Mycenaeans were trading as early as the 16th century BC. At first, they had to compete with the Minoans, but they found more trading opportunities as Cretan power declined.

The Mycenaeans traded extensively in the eastern Mediterranean and kept trading posts in important cities along the coasts of Asia Minor and Lebanon. They also purchased items from more distant lands, such as Africa or Scandinavia, through other traders.

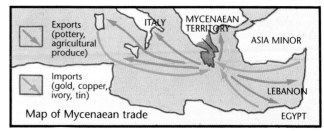

Exports (pottery, agricultural produce)

Imports (gold, copper, ivory, tin)

ITALY
MYCENAEAN TERRITORY
ASIA MINOR
LEBANON
EGYPT

Map of Mycenaean trade

Houses

Store rooms

Workshops for craftsmen

Royal palace

Storerooms

Agricultural produce from the surrounding area was kept in storerooms on the *acropolis* to be used or exported. Imported goods and objects made by craft workers were also stored there.

Pots from Mycenae

Craft workshops

The king employed many artists and craft workers. They had workshops on the *acropolis*, where they produced goods such as pots, statuettes, jewels, cloth and weapons. These objects were used by the household, given to employees as payment for work, or exported for profit.

The royal palace

A Mycenaean palace consisted of a number of buildings around a central courtyard. It was brightly painted, both inside and out. The king held court and conducted state business in a large hall known as a *megaron*. Little remains of the *megaron* at Mycenae. This reconstruction is based on the remains from other palaces, which would have been similar.

The room contained four pillars and a hearth.

The walls were covered with frescoes.

Warriors

The Mycenaeans seem to have been a very warlike people. We know from the weapons and equipment found in graves that their kings and nobles were warriors. A ruler was expected to take care of his soldiers, supplying them with food, housing, land and slaves. This was organized through the palace, where many warriors lived.

Mycenaean soldiers used helmets and shields. Various helmets are shown on vases and frescoes. Most had cheek flaps and were fastened under the chin. Bronze plates were also worn for body protection.

This bronze suit was found in a grave. The leather helmet is covered with the tusks of wild boars.

The Mycenaeans used three types of shields: a rectangular tower shape, an eight shape and a round shape. They were made of oxhide leather on a wooden frame. Poorer soldiers wore leather tunics to protect themselves.

The foot soldiers on this vase are wearing leather tunics.

We know very little about how armies were organized, but it seems that rulers and nobles fought from chariots.

Each chariot probably contained a driver and a warrior.

The Trojan War

The story of the Trojan War is told in the *Iliad*, a poem thought to have been written by the Greek poet, Homer. It describes how a city called Troy was destroyed by the Greeks after a ten year siege. For many years, historians thought that the Trojan War was just a story. But in the 19th century AD, the remains of Troy were discovered in modern Turkey. We still cannot prove that the Trojan War happened exactly as the *Iliad* describes. But a war may have taken place around 1250BC, and this may have inspired the poet of the *Iliad*.

Reconstruction showing the city of Troy under siege from the Greeks

The legend of the Trojan War

The cause of the war between Greece and Troy was Helen of Sparta. She was so beautiful that all the Greek kings wanted to marry her. Helen eventually married Menelaus, brother of King Agamemnon of Mycenae. Her father made all her suitors swear to support Menelaus and to help if anyone tried to kidnap Helen.

Unfortunately, Aphrodite, the goddess of love and beauty, promised Helen to Paris, a prince of Troy. She made Helen fall in love with him, and the pair eloped to Troy. Agamemnon was angry. He reminded the Greek kings of their oath, and organized a military expedition to Troy, to get Helen back.

Troy was a heavily fortified city and could not easily be defeated. For ten years, the Greeks laid siege to the city. Then Odysseus, the king of Ithaca, thought of a trick to help them seize Troy.

They built a huge wooden horse, left it outside the city and then sailed away. When they had gone, the Trojans brought the horse into the city, thinking it would bring them luck.

That night, Greek soldiers, who were concealed inside the hollow horse, crept out and opened the city gates. The Greek army, which had sneaked back under cover of darkness, charged in and destroyed the city. They killed the men and made the women and children slaves. Only one Trojan prince, Aeneas, escaped alive with his family. He fled to Italy, where his descendants are said to have founded the city of Rome.

The search for Troy

At the end of the 19th century AD, a German archaeologist named Heinrich Schliemann set out to discover the city of Troy. He had complete faith in Homer and the *Iliad*, and used the descriptions in the poem to locate the city.

A picture of the wooden horse, taken from a Greek vase

In AD1870, Schliemann started to dig at a site at Hisarlik, in modern Turkey. He uncovered the ruins of a city which he believed to be Troy. Several archaeologists have since excavated the site. We now know that the city was built around 3600BC, but it was rebuilt at least eight times. Experts disagree about which of the layers is the city described in the *Iliad*.

Several of the cities uncovered at Hisarlik were destroyed violently, but we do not know whether this was by earthquake or war. People from the Greek mainland may well have destroyed the city, but there is not yet any evidence to prove that the Trojan War took place as the *Iliad* describes.

For a link to a website where you can find out more about the Trojan War, go to www.usborne-quicklinks.com

The end of the age

Egyptian records show that in the 13th century BC there was a long run of poor harvests followed by famine. In Mycenaean Greece, bad harvests would also have affected trade, as agricultural produce was exported and the profits used to pay workers. Without it, the whole economic system and way of life was threatened (see diagram on the right).

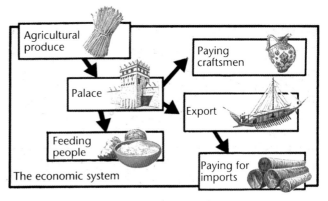
The economic system

A Mycenaean trading party

In times of shortage, the Mycenaeans traditionally attacked nearby cities to steal cattle and crops. Huge walls were built around many cities at this time and these may well have been built as protection against attack. Some Mycenaeans may also have gone on raids overseas. This may have been the real cause of the war against Troy.

The Sea Peoples

Egyptian texts show that around 1190BC emigrants were reported in the eastern Mediterranean. Some journeyed overland, while others were at sea in a battle fleet. The Egyptians named them the Sea Peoples. Some of the Sea Peoples seem to have been Mycenaean refugees, driven out by the famine.

A reconstruction of a battle between the Egyptians and the Sea Peoples, based on an Egyptian carving.

Map of the Sea Peoples' route

ITALY
ASIA MINOR
GREECE
CYPRUS
PALESTINE
Sea Peoples' fleet
Sea Peoples' army
Route after defeat
EGYPT
Sea Peoples defeated off Egypt, c.1183BC

The Sea Peoples' fleet seized Cyprus, while their army destroyed several cities. The fleet and army were eventually defeated by the Egyptian Pharaoh Ramesses III. After this the Sea Peoples dispersed around the Mediterranean. Some may have been the ancestors of the Etruscans in Italy and of the Philistines in Palestine.

The Dorians

One by one, the Mycenaean cities were abandoned. Some may have been ruined by earthquakes, others were destroyed by enemies. As the Mycenaean world disintegrated, Greece entered the Dark Ages (see page 16) and a people known as the Dorians came to prominence.

It was once thought that the Dorians invaded from outside Greece. However, experts now think that they had been in Greece for some time, but took advantage of the troubled times to exert their influence. In the places where they settled, the Dorian dialect of Greek was later spoken. Different dialects developed in other areas.

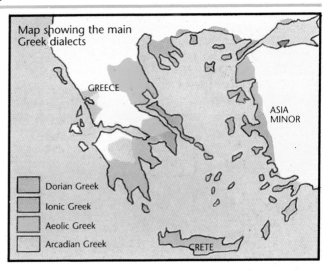
Map showing the main Greek dialects

GREECE
ASIA MINOR
Dorian Greek
Ionic Greek
Aeolic Greek
Arcadian Greek
CRETE

The Dark Ages: c.1100-800BC

This period is known as the Dark Ages, because we know little of what happened in Greece. The art of writing was lost after the end of the Mycenaean civilization, so there are no written records. There is also little mention of the Greeks in foreign records, as they had few contacts with other countries. By the beginning of the Dark Ages, the population had decreased dramatically. There was a decline in the standard of crafts and architecture. Skills such as fresco painting and gem cutting were forgotten.

Many farming communities were destroyed during the disturbances at the end of the Mycenaean period.

Architecture

In the Dark Ages the main building materials were wood and mud brick (mud mixed with straw and left in the sun to dry). These materials do not last as well as stone, so very few buildings have survived. Most people probably lived in small huts like the one shown in the reconstruction below.

Thatched roof

Wooden frame

Mud brick walls

Clothes

Many dress pins from the Dark Ages have been found. This suggests that fashions were very different from the tightly laced Mycenaean clothes. People wore simple tunics, made from rectangular pieces of cloth, fastened at the shoulders with pins. This style is known as the Doric *chiton*.

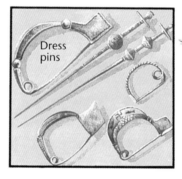

Dress pins

Woman wearing a Doric *chiton*

Burial customs

A cemetery in Athens has revealed that cremation was introduced in the Dark Ages. The body was burned and the ashes were put in a jar in the grave. By around 800BC burial was popular again.

The Mycenaean custom of burying objects with the dead was continued. However, people couldn't usually afford to bury luxury goods and most graves contained just a pottery jug or cup.

This vase painting of a funeral shows the dead person surrounded by mourners who are tearing their hair in grief.

Euboea

On the island of Euboea, excavations have revealed a flourishing Dark Age culture. It was rich enough for people to put gold ornaments in their graves. As early as 900BC, the Euboeans were establishing trading contacts with foreign countries. However, wars between the two main cities on Euboea ended this period of prosperity. The objects below were all discovered in tombs on Euboea.

Terracotta figure of a centaur

Pot decorated with human figures

Gold rings and earrings

Euboea

Athens

The Archaic Period: c.800-500BC

The Archaic Period was a time of progress. The population grew and the standard of living improved.

Art and literature also flourished and the Greeks had more contact with the outside world.

The rediscovery of writing

Around 800BC, the Greeks started to write again. They traded with a people called the Phoenicians, who used an alphabet containing only consonants. The Greeks adapted this by introducing signs for vowels. This system was very successful, and is the basis of the alphabet we use today. The chart on the right shows the letters of the Greek alphabet, the name of each letter and the English sound.

α alpha a	β beta b	γ gamma g	δ delta d	ε epsilon e	ζ zeta z	η eta e	θ theta th
ι iota i	κ kappa k	λ lambda l	μ mu m	ν nu n	ξ xi x/ks	ο omicron o	π pi p
ρ rho r	σ/ς sigma s	τ tau t	υ upsilon u	φ phi f/ph	χ chi ch	ψ psi ps	ω omega o

Bards

A bard reciting his poem

No written records were kept in the Dark Ages, but poetry was passed on by word of mouth. Professional poets, known as bards, went from place to place, telling stories of the gods and heroes. They knew many long poems by heart.

The poet who composed the *Iliad* and the *Odyssey* probably lived around this time, between 850 and 750BC. We know little about his life, but tradition maintains that his name was Homer and that he was blind. The *Iliad* tells the story of the siege of Troy and the *Odyssey* describes the hero Odysseus' journey home from the Trojan War. These poems are the earliest surviving Greek literature. You can read about them on page 84.

Roman bust of Homer, based on a Greek original

Emigration

As the population started to grow, some areas of Greece became overcrowded and sometimes there were famines. Political struggles between the various Greek states also created exiles and refugees, who were forced to flee abroad. From around 1000BC, groups of people left Greece seeking land or employment overseas.

The first emigrants settled in the coastal area of Asia Minor, which was called Ionia. Later groups settled all around the Mediterranean. They chose coastal areas and good farming land, where they faced little opposition from the local inhabitants. Once a colony was established, it rapidly became independent from the mother city.

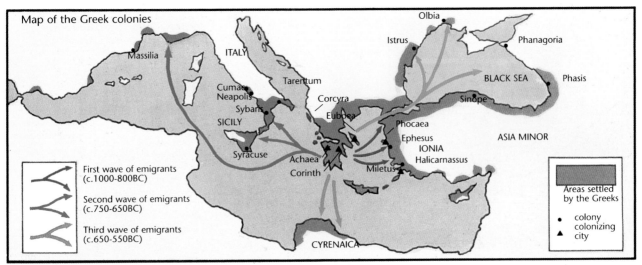
Map of the Greek colonies

First wave of emigrants (c.1000-800BC)
Second wave of emigrants (c.750-650BC)
Third wave of emigrants (c.650-550BC)

Areas settled by the Greeks
colony
colonizing city

The Greeks and the Mediterranean world

During the Dark Ages, the Greeks had little contact with other countries. But, from the Archaic Period, they set up colonies and began to trade.

This brought them into contact with many different countries and peoples around the Mediterranean area. Some are described below.

The Assyrians

During the Dark Ages, a people known as the Assyrians conquered a vast area of the Middle East. They came from the area that is now Iraq, and their most important cities were Ashur (the capital) and Nineveh.

Map of the Assyrian Empire, c.646BC

Nineveh
ASSYRIA • Ashur
MEDITERRANEAN SEA
EGYPT
Assyrian territory

This stone carving shows the Assyrian king Ashurbanipal out hunting.

The Assyrians were a warlike people, famed for their cruelty. Archaeologists have discovered lists of Assyrian kings going back to 2500BC. However, it was not until around 1814BC that they started to expand their territory. Their empire reached its height in around 646BC under King Ashurbanipal.

The Egyptians

There were many trading links between Egypt and the Greeks. The Greeks purchased linen, perfumes, wine and papyrus for scrolls from the Egyptians. They also kept trading posts in the Egyptian cities of Naucratis and Daphnae.

The pyramids at Giza were built in the 26th century BC and were tombs for Egyptian kings.

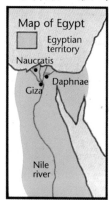

By the time of the Greek Dark Ages, the Egyptian civilization had existed for over 2000 years. In c.1190BC Pharaoh Ramesses III (also known as Ramses III) defeated the Sea Peoples, but under his successors Egyptian power declined. Alexander the Great (see pages 74-75) conquered Egypt, and in 30BC it became part of the Roman Empire.

Map of Egypt
Egyptian territory
Naucratis
Daphnae
Giza
Nile river

The Etruscans

Around 750BC, the Greeks began to set up colonies in southern Italy. There they came into conflict with the Etruscans, who were expanding their territory southward from northwestern Italy. Some experts believe the Etruscans were Italian natives. Others think they were Sea Peoples who had to find a new home after their defeat by the Egyptians.

They may even have come from Asia Minor.

The Etruscans were expert sailors, who traded extensively around the Mediterranean. They were also skilled metalworkers. Their engineers knew how to build sewage systems for their towns and drain marshy areas.

Terracotta head of an Etruscan warrior

Etruscan statue from a temple built in the 3rd century BC

Bronze statue of a mythical beast known as a *chimera*

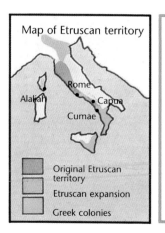

Map of Etruscan territory

Rome
Alaliah • Capua
Cumae

Original Etruscan territory
Etruscan expansion
Greek colonies

Key dates

c.900BC Etruscan cities are founded in northwest Italy.

c.600BC Etruscans found city of Capua and clash with Greek colonists at Cumae.

c.540BC Etruscans defeat the Greeks in a naval battle at Alaliah and gain control of Corsica and the northwest Mediterranean.

474BC Greeks defeat the Etruscans in a naval battle off Cumae. Etruscans lose control of the northwest Mediterranean.

358-262BC Romans conquer the Etruscan cities.

For links to websites where you can find out more about the Scythians and the Etruscans, go to www.usborne-quicklinks.com

The Phoenicians

During the Greek Dark Ages, the most successful traders in the Mediterranean were the Phoenicians. They lived on the coast in what is now the Lebanon. Their most important exports were purple cloth, timber, glass and goods made of metal and wood, including fine furniture inlaid with ivory. They lived in independent city-states, each of which had its own king. Their most important cities were Byblos, Sidon and Tyre.

A Phoenician trading ship leaving port

The Phoenicians were daring sailors and explorers, and established colonies on the south and west shores of the Mediterranean. In around 1000BC they invented a form of writing. Their alphabet was later adopted by the Greeks (see page 17).

Phoenician pots made from patterned glass

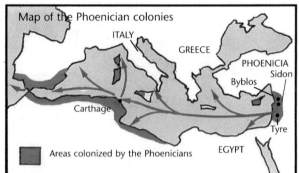

Map of the Phoenician colonies

ITALY

GREECE

PHOENICIA
Sidon

Byblos

Carthage

Tyre

EGYPT

Areas colonized by the Phoenicians

Key dates

c.1200-1000BC Phoenicians rise to power.

c.814BC Princess Elissa of Tyre founds Carthage on the North African coast.

c.600BC Phoenician sailors circumnavigate Africa.

539BC Phoenicia is conquered by the Persians (see page 41).

332BC Phoenicia is conquered by Alexander the Great (see pages 74-75).

The Lydians

Lydian coin

Lydia was a small, wealthy state in Asia Minor. Its capital was Sardis. The Lydians lived close to the Ionian Greek colonies, and traded with them.

Key dates

c.680-652BC Reign of King Gyges. He attacks the Ionian Greek colonies, while trying to maintain relations with Greece.

7th century BC The Lydians are the first people to use coins.

560-546BC Reign of King Croesus. In alliance with a people called the Medes, he conquers the Ionian colonies.

546BC Croesus is defeated by the Persians. The Persians seize the Ionian colonies (see page 40).

The Scythians

The Scythians were a nomadic people from Central Asia who kept herds of horses, cattle and sheep. Around 1000BC, they moved to the area around the Black Sea. They were a warlike people, and Greek colonists who settled around the Black Sea often had to defend their territory against them. But a lot of trade was done between the two peoples. The Greeks bought wheat, salt, hides and slaves from the Scythians.

A Scythian chief, noblewoman and horse

In return they supplied them with metalwork, oils and wines. The Scythians were a very wealthy people. Their graves were filled with rich goods, along with human and horse sacrifices.

Greek metalworkers made many gold ornaments like these for the Scythians.

Key dates

674-650BC The Scythians make an alliance with the Assyrians, then plunder parts of the Middle East.

c.630BC The Scythians defeat the Cimmerians, who are from central Asia.

514BC The Scythians hold back the Persians.

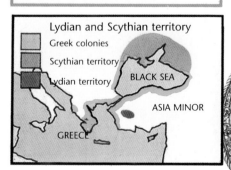

Lydian and Scythian territory

Greek colonies

Scythian territory

Lydian territory

BLACK SEA

ASIA MINOR

GREECE

Earring

Necklace

Ornament for clothes

Vase

Social structure and government

In the Archaic Period, Greece was made up of many independent states. The Greeks referred to each of these as a *polis*, or city-state. A *polis* consisted of the city and its surrounding countryside. At around 2,500 square km (1,000 square miles), Athens was the largest *polis*. Most states were much smaller, many with less than 250 square km (100 square miles).

The Greeks liked to keep each city-state fairly small. Even the largest had no more than a few thousand citizens. The reconstruction on the right shows what a typical *polis* would have looked like during the Archaic Period.

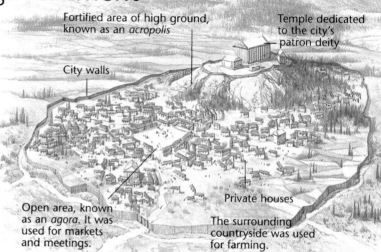

Fortified area of high ground, known as an *acropolis*

Temple dedicated to the city's patron deity

City walls

Private houses

Open area, known as an *agora*. It was used for markets and meetings.

The surrounding countryside was used for farming.

Social structure

In Greek society there were two main groups of people: free people and slaves. Slaves were owned by free people. They were used as servants and had no legal rights. Some were prisoners of war from other Greek states. Others were foreigners bought from slave traders. Many slaves worked closely with their owners and lived as members of the family. A few were skilled craft workers and were paid for their work.

Female slaves doing basic housework

Male slaves at work on a farm

In Athens, as society developed, free men were split into two groups: citizens and *metics*. A citizen was a free man, born to Athenian parents. Citizens were the only people who could take part in the government of the *polis*. They had to serve in the army, and were also expected to volunteer for jury service (see pages 60-61).

A *metic* was a man born outside Athens who had come to live there, usually to trade or to work at a craft. Many *metics* were very prosperous. They had to pay tax and serve in the army if required, but they could never become citizens. They had no say in the government, could not own houses or land and could not speak in court.

Metics often worked as potters or metalworkers.

A man born into one of these social groups could rarely move into another one. The only people who could sometimes improve their social status were slaves.

Occasionally, a master would pay to set a skilled slave up in business. He would receive a share of the profits in return. Some of these slaves were able to save up and buy their freedom. But freed slaves could never become citizens or *metics*.

All these divisions applied only to men. Women took their status from their husband or male relations. They weren't permitted to take part in public life.

A slave receiving his freedom

Changing forms of government

Rule by the aristocrats: c.800-650BC

By the Archaic Period, most Greek states were governed by groups of rich landowners, known as aristocrats. The word comes from the Greek *aristoi*, meaning 'best people'. This system of government is known as an *oligarchy*, which means 'rule by the few' in Greek. As trade increased, a middle class of merchants, craftsmen and bankers began to prosper. But they could not take part in government, and soon began to demand a say in the decision making.

In the early days, aristocrats were the only ones who could afford to buy horses. They became leaders in war and at home.

The age of tyrants: c.650-500BC

Resentment of aristocratic power often led to riots. To establish peace, people sometimes allowed one man to take absolute power. This sort of leader was called a tyrant, meaning 'ruler'. Tyrants first appeared around 650BC. To protect their own positions, they often tried to curb the power of the aristocrats. Some tyrants stayed in power for many years, but most only ruled for a short time.

Tyrants were often deposed by men who envied their power.

Government in Athens: c.750-621BC

During the Archaic Period, real power in Athens lay with the *areopagus*, or council, and with the three magistrates, known as *archons*, who carried out the council's policies. All the *archons* and the members of the council were aristocrats. Many people were dissatisfied with this system and with the city's laws. The Athenians looked for someone to reform their laws, and in 621BC they appointed a man called Draco. He drew up a set of laws which were extremely severe. Today, a harsh rule is still referred to as 'draconian'.

Even minor crimes such as stealing food were punished by death.

Solon's reforms

People were unhappy with Draco's laws. In 594BC an aristocrat named Solon became *archon* and introduced reforms. Many of Solon's measures were very popular. He prevented merchants from selling grain abroad, so there was more food for the poor. He stopped people who were in debt from being sold into slavery. Solon also reformed the system of government, so that men from the middle classes could hold administrative positions. Even poor citizens were given a say in the city's affairs, through an Assembly (see page 60).

Solon arranged for debtors to be freed. Some were brought home from abroad.

The tyrant of Athens

Despite these reforms, few people were satisfied. Solon left Athens and disorder broke out. Around 546BC, an aristocrat named Peisistratus took power. Under his rule, Athens enjoyed a time of peace and prosperity. Peisistratus tried to take power several times. Once he arrived in Athens with a woman dressed as Athene. He tried to persuade people that the goddess had appointed him leader.

Peisistratus in Athens with a woman dressed as Athene.

The introduction of democracy

Peisistratus was succeeded by his son Hippias in 527BC. Hippias was overthrown in 510BC, and civil war followed. Cleisthenes, an aristocrat from the Alcmaeonid family, eventually triumphed. In 508BC he introduced a system of government known as *democracy* (see pages 60-61).

Hippias was deposed by the Alcmaeonid family, helped by Spartan troops.

21

Sparta

In the 10th century BC, the Dorians moved into Laconia, a province of southern Greece. They defeated the native inhabitants and founded the state of Sparta. Between c.740 and 720BC, the Spartans conquered the nearby state of Messenia. This made Sparta one of the largest Greek states and gave it enough fertile land to make it self-sufficient in food.

By the beginning of the Archaic Period, the Spartans were trading with other Greek states and importing luxury goods from abroad. Their craftsmen made fine metalware and painted vases. The Spartans are said to have played a leading role in the invention of Greek music, and Alcman, a Spartan poet, became very well known.

Map of Spartan state

Bronze figure of a Spartan warrior, 5th century BC

This scene is from a Spartan pot known as the Vix *krater* (see page 48). It dates from the 6th century BC and shows Spartan soldiers marching to war.

In 668BC, the Spartans were defeated in a war against Argos. Then, around 630BC, the Messenians started a revolt against the Spartans, which lasted for 17 years. These events convinced the Spartans that they must make drastic changes in order to keep the rebellious population under control and to defend themselves against foreign invasion.

They set up a system dedicated to producing warriors. Every male Spartan had to become a full-time soldier, and spent his life training and fighting. Spartans lived in very hard and uncomfortable conditions. They had as little contact with the outside world as possible.

By the Classical Period, Sparta had become the strongest military power in Greece, and its soldiers were famous for their bravery. But this was achieved at the expense of its cultural development. There were now no philosophers or artists in Sparta.

This Spartan plate was made in c.560BC.

Social structure

Only men of Spartan birth were regarded as citizens. They were an exclusive group who never admitted any outsiders. All citizens served in the army and could vote in the assembly.

Men who were not citizens were known as *perioikoi*. They were free men who were allowed to trade and serve in the army. *Perioikoi* and their families lived in separate small villages around Sparta.

Helots were descendants of Sparta's original inhabitants. They farmed the land and had to give part of their crops to their Spartan masters. The Spartans kept the *helots* oppressed, to prevent rebellions.

Life in Sparta

Physical fitness was important, as only strong, healthy men could be soldiers. Each new baby was examined by officials. If it showed signs of weakness, it was left to die.

A boy was educated until he was 20 (see pages 52-53). Then he had to join the army and be elected to a military club. He lived in the club's barracks in very harsh conditions.

Soldiers were allocated land, and *helots* to work it, by the state. Each soldier supported his family and helped to supply his barracks from the produce of his land.

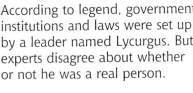

Spartan men didn't usually marry until they were 30. Even then they spent most of their time at the barracks. Only old men were allowed to live in their own homes.

Women had to keep fit so they would have strong babies. They competed against each other in athletic events, wearing short tunics. Other Greeks were often shocked by this.

Foreigners were not allowed into Sparta. Only the *perioikoi* had any dealings with outsiders. The Spartans did not use coins and usually bartered for goods.

Government in Sparta

The Spartan government included a monarchy, a council of elders and a popular assembly. Their various functions are shown on this diagram.

According to legend, government institutions and laws were set up by a leader named Lycurgus. But experts disagree about whether or not he was a real person.

Sparta had two royal families and two kings, who always ruled together. Their main responsibility was to lead the army in war. At home, their powers were strictly limited to religious duties.

More actual power lay with the five *ephors*, or overseers, who were elected annually by the Assembly (see below). They looked after the day-to-day running of the state.

The *gerousia*, or Council, was made up of the two kings and 20 councillors. Councillors were men over 60 who had been elected for life by the Assembly. The councillors decided which policies Sparta should adopt. They also created the laws and acted as judges.

The Council's proposals had to be passed by the *apella*, or Assembly, which consisted of all citizens over 30. The Assembly could not debate or amend a measure, it could only vote on it. Spartans voted by shouting 'yes' or 'no': the loudest group won.

The Peloponnesian League

The Spartans didn't have enough soldiers to fight abroad and suppress a *helot* uprising at the same time. In the 6th century BC, they made alliances with the peoples of the Peloponnese (the southern part of mainland Greece). This is known as the Peloponnesian League. Sparta's allies remained independent, but they had to give Sparta military assistance when required.

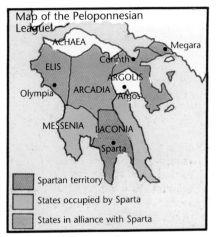

Map of the Peloponnesian League

- Spartan territory
- States occupied by Sparta
- States in alliance with Sparta

For a link to a website where you can find out more about the differences between Athens and Sparta, go to **www.usborne-quicklinks.com**

Farming and food

Most people in ancient Greece made their living from farming. Even the citizens of towns often had farms, which provided their income. However, around three-quarters of the land area of Greece was mountainous and of little use for agriculture.

Land could be farmed on the coastal plain and in some inland areas, and in places the soil was very fertile. Only a few areas, such as Thessaly, had good pasture land. Very little rain fell between March and October, so crops were grown during the winter.

A Greek farm

This scene shows a typical Greek farm. They were usually quite small, and only produced enough food to support a single family. Farms were worked by the owner, his family and a few hired hands or slaves. If the owner lived in the town, he paid a servant to run the farm.

Areas of high ground or poor soil, which were useless for other crops, were used to grow olive trees.

Grapes were grown in vineyards on the lower hill slopes.

Farm buildings

Grain was grown on the fertile plains. It was the most important crop, as bread was the main part of the Greek diet.

Farmers grew fruit and vegetables to feed their families.

Many farmers kept animals, which grazed on the hillsides. Herders took care of them.

Farm animals

Farmers kept animals for their milk and meat. They were also used for work, and their hides provided leather.

Horses were expensive to keep and were usually only used by the rich.

Oxen and mules were used to pull heavy farm equipment.

Fish were plentiful in the seas around Greece.

Farmers often kept pigs and poultry for their meat.

In fertile areas cows were kept for their milk.

Most milk came from sheep and goats. They were also eaten, and their hides were used for leather.

Grapes

Grapes were picked in September. Some were kept for eating, but most were made into wine. They were trodden underfoot in big vats. This first squeezing of the grapes made the best quality wine. The juice was then left in jars to ferment.

Olives

An olive press

The picture on this vase shows an olive harvest.

Olives were picked by hand, or knocked out of the trees with sticks. Some were eaten, but most were crushed in a press to make oil. Olive oil was an essential product. It was used for cooking, lighting and in beauty products. In Athens it was a crime to uproot an olive tree.

The grain harvest

1. Grain was sown in October, so that it could grow during the wettest months of the year. The earth had to be turned over to loosen it. Then the seeds could be sown, to grow during the winter and spring.

2. In April or May, crops were harvested with curved knives, known as sickles. After the harvest, the field was left unplanted for a while so that the soil could rest and regain its natural nutrients.

3. The harvest was threshed to separate the grain from the stalks. Mules trampled the crop on a paved floor. Some floors were positioned so that the wind would also blow away the chaff, the grain's outer cover.

4. Sometimes, the grain was thrown in the air, so that the light chaff would blow away. This is known as winnowing. The husks were then removed by beating the grain with a heavy pounder.

What people ate

Most people in Greece lived mainly on porridge and bread. This was usually barley bread, as wheat was more expensive than barley. Other common foods were cheese, fish, vegetables, eggs and fruit. Wild animals such as hares, deer and boar were hunted to supplement the food supply. A typical day's food is shown on the right.

Coriander and sesame were popular seasonings. Bees were kept in terracotta hives to provide honey, the only form of sweetening.

Rich people had a far more varied diet. They ate more fish and meat and could afford bread made from wheat.

Breakfast was usually a lump of bread soaked in wine.

The main meal of the day was often barley porridge or bread with some vegetables.

Bread, with a piece of cheese, or some olives and figs, was a typical lunch.

A Greek house

Very few Greek houses have survived, so we can't be sure exactly what a typical house looked like. We do know that houses were usually built around a central courtyard from which doors opened into the various ground floor rooms. Any windows on the outside walls of the house tended to be small and could be closed with shutters. This made the house very private and secure. Stairs led from the courtyard to the upper floor, where the bedrooms and servants' quarters were situated. Men and women lived separate lives and had separate rooms within the house.

This reconstruction is based on the remains of a house found in the city of Olynthos. Some walls have been cut away to show the layout of the rooms. Not all the activities shown in this picture would have happened at the same time.

The roof was made of pottery tiles.

The women's quarters were known as the *gynaeceum*. Women spent most of their time in these rooms, organizing the household, spinning, weaving and entertaining their friends.

The exterior

Outside walls were built from mud bricks, sometimes reinforced with timber. These bricks were cheap and easy to use, but they were not very strong. Burglars broke into houses by burrowing through the walls. Doors and shutters were made of wood with bronze hinges. Wood was a valuable material, as it was very scarce.

A statue of the god Hermes, known as a *herm*, often stood by the main entrance to the house to ward off evil. Wealthy people often employed a doorman to receive visitors.

Herm

The men ate and entertained their friends in a room called the *andron*.

Mosaic floors were used in some rooms. They were made from pebbles.

Heating was provided by burning charcoal in portable metal braziers.

Furniture

Furniture was usually made of wood. Rich people had more highly decorated furniture. It was often finely carved with inlays of ivory, gold and silver. Some items were made of bronze.

Chairs

Most people sat on stools, but the master of the house used a *thronos*, a large chair with arms. Ladies used chairs with backs. This style was called a *klismos*.

Klismos

Thronos   Stool

Tables

Tables were usually low, so they could be pushed under couches when not in use. They had three legs, or a single, central support.

Slaves' room

Walls were usually painted in a plain shade. They were often hung with bright, patterned tapestries, which were made by the women of the household.

The kitchen contained an open fire used for cooking. Sometimes there was a chimney shaft, to allow smoke to escape.

Altar

Bedroom

The bathroom contained a terracotta tub with a drain which led outside. There was a basin on a stand for washing.

The courtyard usually contained an altar where prayers were said. Some courtyards also had a well to supply water.

The family gathered together in a comfortable room with a fire. This room was dedicated to the hearth goddess, Hestia.

Couches and beds

Beds and couches were similar in design. They had a wooden frame, strung with leather thongs or cords. On top of this was a mattress, pillows and a cover.

Storage

Small boxes or baskets were used for storing small personal items, such as jewels. Larger items, such as clothes or bed linen, were stored in chests.

Lighting

Small oil-burning lamps made of pottery, bronze or silver lit the rooms. The oil was put in the round body of the lamp, with a wick in the spout. Lamps could be placed on special bronze stands to raise them.

Clothes and fashion

Greek clothes were very simple. Both men and women wore pieces of material around their bodies in the form of a tunic or cloak. This material was usually wool or linen, but in the 5th century BC, the Greeks also began to use cotton, from India.

By the 4th century BC, silk was being made on the island of Kos, and other luxury cloths were imported. Only the rich could afford these exotic materials. The poor used simpler materials, such as undyed or unbleached wool and linen.

Women's clothes

The basic female dress was known as a *chiton*. It was made from a rectangular piece of cloth.

There were two main styles of *chiton*, the Doric and the Ionic.

The *chiton* was fastened with buttons or brooches.

A girdle could be tied around the waist.

The *chiton* was fastened at intervals on the shoulders.

A girdle was often tied around the waist.

A *himation* could be a light, gauzy scarf.

This cloak was also a *himation*.

For a Doric *chiton*, the top quarter of material was folded over and then wrapped around the body.

The Ionic style of *chiton* was thought to have been invented in the Greek colonies in Ionia.

Women also wore a rectangular-shaped wrap, known as a *himation*. These varied in size and thickness.

Changing fashions

Costly materials had gold ornaments sewn on.

Paintings on vases show that in the Archaic Period highly patterned, bright fabrics were fashionable and women's dresses usually clung closely to the body.

In later years, dresses were in one shade, but sometimes had a contrasting band or a small pattern along the edge. The garments were looser by this time.

In the 4th century BC this trend was reversed. Patterned materials were in fashion again. The materials were fine and clung more revealingly to the figure.

Men's clothes

Young men wore thigh-length tunics.

Old men and the rich wore ankle-length tunics.

Slave wearing a loincloth

Greek men wore a simple kilt or a tunic sewn up at the side and fastened on one or both shoulders. Craftsmen and slaves often wore a loincloth.

Men also wore a *himation*. It was usually rectangular in shape but varied considerably in size and texture. Sometimes it was worn over a tunic. It was wrapped around the body with the end thrown over one shoulder.

There was also a shorter cloak, known as a *chlamys*, which was usually worn by younger men, particularly for hunting or riding, or by soldiers. It was fastened with a pin or brooch.

Chlamys

Himation

Footwear

Leather sandal

Leather boot

Leather shoe

For a link to a web site where you can view an album of pictures of ancient Greek jewels, with details of how they were made, go to **www.usborne-quicklinks.com**

Many people went barefoot most of the time, especially indoors. Leather sandals were the most usual footwear, although shoes were sometimes worn. Horsemen wore calf-length boots with open toes.

Hats

Both men and women wore hats with brims when they were outdoors, to protect themselves from the sun.

Jewels

Many Greek jewels have survived in tombs, as it was the custom to bury dead people with their ornaments. Paintings, sculptures and lists from temples give us other details. Rich people had jewels made of gold, silver, electrum and ivory. Poorer people had to make do with bronze, lead, iron, bone and glass.

Greek goldsmiths worked gold into many different shapes and textures, and sometimes added touches of enamel for variety. Gemstones were not used until the Hellenistic period.

Clasp

Gold headband, called a diadem, c.350BC

Gold necklace, from the Classical Period

Gold bracelet, decorated with lion heads, c.350BC

Gold earrings, c.350BC

Gold ring in the shape of a snake, from the Classical Period

Hairstyles

In the Archaic Period, men wore their hair long and had full beards.

Hair styles and beards became shorter during the Classical Period.

In the Hellenistic Period, it was fashionable to be clean-shaven.

In the Archaic Period women wore their hair long, in a headband.

In the Classical Period, hair was worn up with ribbons, nets or scarves.

In the Hellenistic Period curls were in fashion. Hair was still usually worn up.

Pottery

Although Greek pottery was intended for everyday use, it was often painted with beautiful designs.

The pictures on many pots have given us vital information about how the Greeks lived.

Styles of decoration

The Geometric Period: c.1000-700BC

In the Dark Ages, simple geometric patterns replaced the fish and plant decorations of the Bronze Age. Very elaborate geometric patterns were common around 900BC. In the 9th and 8th centuries BC, bands of decoration featuring animals and humans were added. Figures were shown as silhouettes against a light background.

Funeral scene with animals and humans

Early Dark Age design

Later, more elaborate geometric design

The Orientalizing and Archaic Periods: c.720-550BC

Jug with oriental design

As the Greeks started to have more contact with other countries, oriental motifs such as lotus plants, palm trees, lions and monsters became common on pottery. In the Archaic Period, scenes from Greek mythology and from everyday life began to appear on pots. The figures were more detailed and less formal than those of the Geometric period.

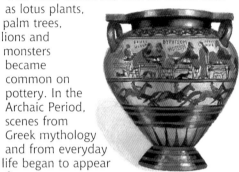
Pot with detailed figures

Athenian pottery: c.550-300BC

Athenian pottery dominated the market for over 200 years. Pictures on Athenian pots showed scenes from the lives of gods and heroes, and scenes from daily life.

At first, the Athenians made black figure ware: red pots decorated with black figures. This style was fashionable from around 550-480BC.

Black figure ware

In around 530BC the Athenians developed red figure ware: black pots decorated with red figures. This eventually replaced the black figure style of pot.

The Athenians also produced white pots with painted decorations, like the one shown on the right.

Red figure ware

The Hellenistic Period: from c.300BC

In the Hellenistic Period, black and red figure ware were rarely made and plain pots, often with raised patterns, like this one, became the most usual style.

Pot from the Hellenistic Period

Identifying shapes

Pots were made in many different shapes and sizes according to their use. Some of the most popular styles are shown here.

Kraters were large vases in which wine was mixed with water before it was served.

— *Volute krater*

Calyx krater

An *amphora* was a two-handled storage jar with a wide body and narrow neck. *Amphorae* were used to store wine, oil and many other liquids, and they varied greatly in size and shape.

The mixture of water and wine was transferred to a jug known as an *oinochoe*, ready for pouring.

How pots were made

Greek potters were skilled craftsmen who made a variety of things, including large storage jars, fine black and red figure ware, cooking pots, lamps and perhaps even roof tiles. The more decorative pots were usually mde by two people: the potter and the artist who painted them, although sometimes one man did both jobs.

Pots were often signed on the bottom by both the potter and the artist.

In Athens, the potters had their own quarter, which was known as the *Kerameikos*. Potters' workshops were usually small and employed only five or six men. This reconstruction shows the inside of a typical workshop.

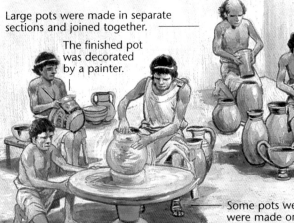

Large pots were made in separate sections and joined together.

The finished pot was decorated by a painter.

Pots were fired (baked) in a kiln like this one, which has been cut away to show how it worked.

Air vent

The finished pot was turned upside down and smoothed, to produce a fine surface.

Some pots were shaped by hand, but most were made on a wheel. An apprentice often turned the wheel for the potter.

Wood or charcoal was burned here to heat the kiln.

Making black and red figure ware

This type of pottery was made from clay that turned red when fired. The areas of the pot that were to be black were painted with a paint made from clay, water and wood ash.

On black figure ware, details could be carved into the black surface so that they would show through in red. Touches of white and dark red paint were used for extra details.

At a point in the firing, all the vents and openings in the kiln were shut. This cut off the oxygen supply and caused a chemical reaction, which turned the whole pot black.

The temperature was then allowed to drop and the vents were reopened. The areas painted with the black slip stayed black, but the rest of the pot turned a clear red.

Skyphos

Water was fetched from the fountain in a *hydria*.

Flasks like these were used for perfume, perfumed oil and ointments.

The *loutrophoros* vase was used to bring water for a bride's ceremonial bath (see page 50).

A special type of *amphora*, filled with oil, was given as a prize for each event at the Panathenaic Games. It was decorated with a picture of the event.

Kylix

Kantharos

The *kantharos*, *kylix* and *skyphos* were all drinking cups.

Makeup box called a *pyxis*

Markets, money and trade

In early times there was no money. People simply exchanged goods for other goods. Coins were probably invented at the end of the 7th century BC in Lydia, in Asia Minor (see page 19). The first coins were made of electrum, a natural mixture of gold and silver. Coins soon spread to the Ionian Greek colonies and then to the Greek mainland.

People gradually came to prefer solid gold or silver coins. The Greeks used silver for most of their coins and a round, flat shape became standard. It became a sign of a city's independence to issue its own coins. The one exception to this was Sparta, where iron rods were used instead of coins until the 4th century BC.

Greek coins

Early electrum coin from Ionia, marked with parallel lines, c.650-600BC

Electrum *stater*, a coin from Lydia, showing a lion and a bull, c.561-545BC

The first coins were small lumps of electrum, stamped with official marks to show that their weight and purity were guaranteed by the state.

Athenian coin showing an owl (Athene's sacred bird)

Stater from Corinth showing Pegasus, the winged horse

From 600-480BC animals were the most popular image on coins. They were usually the symbol of the city that issued the coin.

Coin from Katane in Sicily showing Apollo, c.405BC

Coin from Herakleia, showing Herakles, early 4th century BC

By 480BC, coin-making techniques had greatly improved and the human face and body were shown. Coins usually depicted a god or hero.

Gold coin from Macedonia depicting Philip II, 359-336BC

Coin from Macedonia, showing Alexander the Great, 336-323BC

In the Hellenistic Period, the quality of the designs on coins declined. One new development was to show portraits of rulers.

Trade

Most trade was done by private merchants who sailed from port to port, buying and selling goods. The states did not normally interfere, except to charge custom duties. There was a great deal of trade between the various states within Greece and with the colonies. The colonies also acted as staging posts for Greek trade with the rest of the world.

In the Classical Period, Athens was at the heart of Greek trade, with Corinth a close rival. Areas became associated with particular products: for example, Thessaly and Macedonia exported horses, while Athens exported honey and silver. The main Greek exports were oil, wine, pots, statues, metalwork, cloth and books.

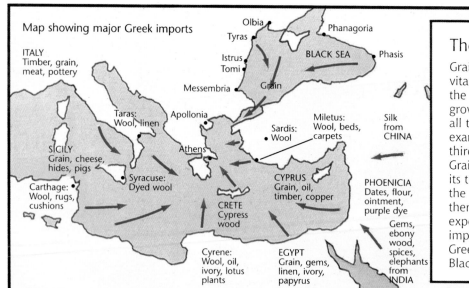

Map showing major Greek imports

ITALY
Timber, grain, meat, pottery

Olbia
Phanagoria
Tyras
Istrus
Tomi
BLACK SEA
Phasis
Messembria
Grain

Taras:
Wool, linen
Apollonia

Miletus:
Wool, beds, carpets

Silk from CHINA

Sardis:
Wool

SICILY
Grain, cheese, hides, pigs

Athens

Carthage:
Wool, rugs, cushions

Syracuse:
Dyed wool

CYPRUS
Grain, oil, timber, copper

PHOENICIA
Dates, flour, ointment, purple dye

CRETE
Cypress wood

Gems, ebony wood, spices, elephants from INDIA

Cyrene:
Wool, oil, ivory, lotus plants

EGYPT
Grain, gems, linen, ivory, papyrus

The grain trade

Grain was the most vital import, as many of the city-states could not grow enough of it to feed all their citizens. Athens, for example, had to import two-thirds of the grain it needed. Grain was so important that its trade was controlled by the state, and at one time there was a death penalty for exporting it. Much of the imported grain came from the Greek colonies around the Black Sea.

Markets

In the middle of every Greek city was the *agora*, a market place. It was the heart of the city's trading activity, and it was also a popular meeting place. Farmers and other merchants came to sell their produce. They set up their stalls in the middle of the *agora*. Customers could buy meat, fish, vegetables, cheese, fruit, eggs and hens. This picture shows what a typical *agora* would have looked like.

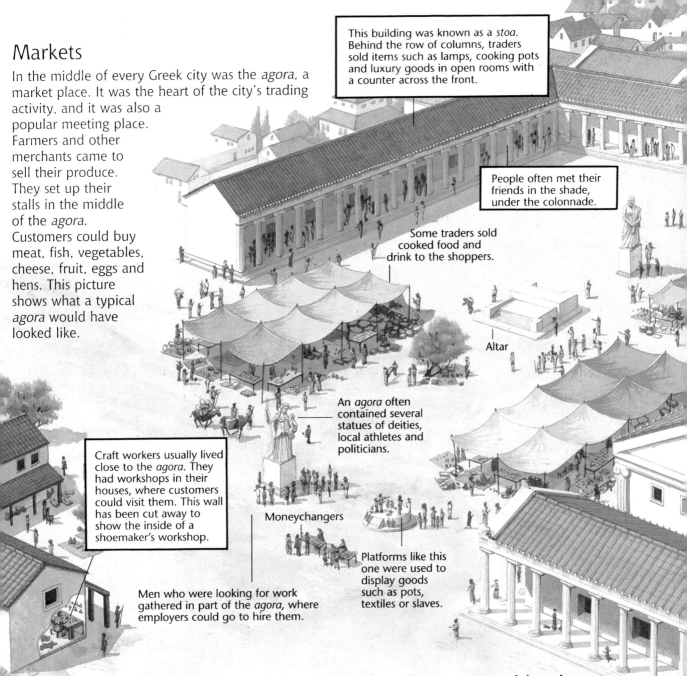

This building was known as a *stoa*. Behind the row of columns, traders sold items such as lamps, cooking pots and luxury goods in open rooms with a counter across the front.

People often met their friends in the shade, under the colonnade.

Some traders sold cooked food and drink to the shoppers.

Altar

An *agora* often contained several statues of deities, local athletes and politicians.

Craft workers usually lived close to the *agora*. They had workshops in their houses, where customers could visit them. This wall has been cut away to show the inside of a shoemaker's workshop.

Moneychangers

Platforms like this one were used to display goods such as pots, textiles or slaves.

Men who were looking for work gathered in part of the *agora*, where employers could go to hire them.

Weights and measures

Traders in and around the *agora* were controlled by officials known as *metronomoi*. In Athens, ten were chosen each year to check weights and measures. Officials known as *agoranomoi* checked the quality of goods, and *sitophylakes* controlled grain trade.

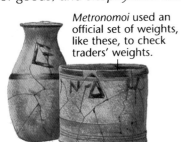

Metronomoi used an official set of weights, like these, to check traders' weights.

Moneychangers and bankers

Each city-state issued its own coins, so people who wanted to trade with another city had to go to a moneychanger. They charged a fee and often made so much profit that they were able to lend money. This was the start of banking. A borrower had to pay back his loan, with interest, by a set date. If he failed to pay he would lose whatever he had pledged to guarantee the loan. This could be his house or his land. People with spare money could also use a banker. He would find a venture to invest it in and would pay the investor interest from the profits.

Moneychangers worked at tables set up in the *agora*.

Travel by land and sea

As Greece is a very mountainous country, land travel was very difficult in ancient times. One of the easiest and quickest ways to travel was by boat. People could pay to travel on one of the merchant ships which sailed around the coast. But sea travel had its risks too, as dishonest sailors sometimes robbed their passengers.

Ships could also be becalmed or driven off course by the wind. To ensure a safe voyage, a sensible captain always made a sacrifice to the sea god Poseidon before sailing. Ships were also at risk from pirates. It was only in the 5th century BC, when Athenian naval power was at its height, that the number of pirates in the Aegean Sea was reduced.

Merchant ships

Several wrecks of merchant ships have been found and excavated by underwater archaeologists. This reconstruction of a trading ship is based on a wreck from around 300BC, which was discovered off Cyprus.

The ship had a large, square sail made of linen.

The mast was made of spruce and the hull of pine. This timber had to be imported from Thrace and Macedonia.

Ropes were made of flax or hemp.

The ship's cargo was stored below the deck.

Two rudder oars at the back were used to steer the ship.

Anchors

Early anchors were made from stones. They had a hole in the top for a rope. The modern shape of anchor was invented by a Greek man named Anacharsis.

Navigating techniques

Merchant ships often sailed very long distances across the sea, which required very good sailing and navigating skills. A Greek man from Miletus, named Thales, studied the Egyptian methods of astronomy and land surveying. He used these to devise a method by which a sea captain could calculate his distance from land, and a system of navigating by the stars. Anaximander, who lived in the 6th century BC, is said to have been the first person to draw a map of the world. Unfortunately, this map has not survived.

The kerkouros

Merchant ships normally relied on sail-power, but writers describe a ship known as a *kerkouros*, which had both a sail and oars. It had a ram at the front which could be used to fight pirate ships. This picture from a vase painting probably shows one.

Greek explorers

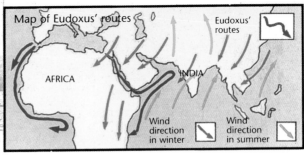

Map of Eudoxus' routes

Eudoxus' routes

AFRICA

INDIA

Wind direction in winter

Wind direction in summer

In around 325-300BC, a Greek man named Pytheas set out from Massilia (modern Marseilles) to explore northward. He landed in Cornwall and then tried to sail around Britain. After sailing north for six days, he reached another island. Experts aren't sure where this was. He wrote an account of his voyage, but most Greeks didn't believe his tales.

Around 110BC, Eudoxus of Cyzicus visited Egypt where he met an Indian sailor. Eudoxus persuaded the man to take him on the trip back to India. He discovered that the monsoon winds carried ships to India from May to September. Then, from November to March, they blew in the other direction and took ships back to Africa.

Land travel

Travel by land was not easy, as the country was very mountainous. The only good roads led to religious sites such as Eleusis (see page 69).

Elsewhere, the roads were often in poor condition. Wars between the Greek states also forced people to make long detours in order to travel safely.

When most ordinary Greeks went on a journey they had to walk.

Carts could only be used where there was a road, or at least a reasonable surface, to run on.

Rich people often rode on horseback.

Merchants carrying goods on uneven tracks or over hilly ground used mules and donkeys as pack animals.

Many roads were a target for bandits.

Staying the night

People often stayed with relatives or friends along their route. There were inns on main roads, but many didn't serve food, so people had to take supplies. In towns, it was possible to sleep in the porches of public buildings, but in remote areas there was little shelter.

In some busy areas, there were hotels, known as *katagogia*. But these were often reserved for important visitors. This is a reconstruction of a hotel which has been found at Epidaurus. It had 160 rooms around four courtyards and was on two floors.

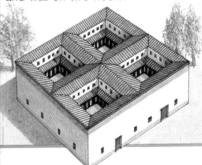

The army

At the beginning of the Archaic Period, the most important part of a Greek army was the cavalry. Warriors had to provide their own equipment, so rich aristocrats dominated the army, as they were the only ones who could afford a horse and the best weapons. Foot soldiers came from the poorer classes, so their equipment was of lower quality.

Statue of a mounted warrior

Later in the Archaic Period, trade increased and the middle classes began to prosper. They could now afford good equipment, and became heavily armed foot soldiers, known as *hoplites*. By the 7th century BC, foot soldiers were the most important part of the army.

A group of hoplite soldiers

A hoplite's equipment

Most armies did not have a uniform, but in later years some standard elements were adopted to make soldiers recognizable in battle. Spartan hoplites always wore scarlet and the Athenians had shields decorated with the letter 'A', for example.

Shields were large enough to protect the body from neck to thigh. A hoplite could choose the decoration on his shield and often used a symbol of his family or city.

Helmets were made of bronze and often had horsehair crests on top. Some popular styles are shown here.

Hoplites wore a jointed breast and back plate called a *cuirass*.

The legs on this shield were the emblem of — a family in Athens.

Early cuirass made of bronze

Later, more flexible cuirass of leather

Illyrian helmet

Attic helmet

Corinthian helmet

A hoplite normally carried a long spear and a short, iron sword.

Thracian helmet

Hoplites wore bronze leg guards, known as greaves.

How the army was organized

Each state had its own procedures for raising and leading its army. In Athens, a man went on to the active service list at 20 and could be called up when there was a war. Men of 50-60 went on to the reserve list and were used for garrison duties. In an emergency, both young men and veterans might have to fight.

The Athenian forces were led by commanders, known as *strategoi*, one from each of the ten Athenian tribes. Only one or two *strategoi* were sent with each expedition. Each of the ten tribes had to provide soldiers for one *phyle*, or regiment, of the army.

In Athens, young men of 18 had to do two years' military training. They were known as *ephebes*.

Battle tactics

As hoplite soldiers began to dominate Greek armies, new battle tactics were needed and methods of fighting changed completely. In the Bronze Age, warriors fought individually. But hoplite soldiers fought in organized formations which required precise training.

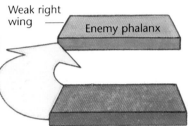

Hoplites fought in a unit known as a phalanx: a long block of soldiers. When a soldier in the front was killed, the man behind took his place.

Exposed side

Each hoplite was protected partly by his own shield and partly by the one next to him. But the man on the right-hand end was left half exposed.

To attack, a phalanx charged into the enemy. If the enemy didn't give way, the two phalanxes had to push until one line broke.

Weak right wing — Enemy phalanx

The right wing of the phalanx was vulnerable because the soldiers were partly unprotected. A general would try to attack the enemy on this side.

For a phalanx to work, the men had to stay in line and move as a unit. They used flute music to help keep in step, as this painting shows.

Thracian soldiers

In the 5th century BC, the Greeks fought against Thracian soldiers, known as *peltasts*. Their tactics were to dash out from cover and hurl javelins into a phalanx. When the phalanx formation was broken, the *peltasts* would pick off individual hoplites. To fight them, the Greeks used fit soldiers known as *ekdromoi*, or 'runners out', who would run out of the phalanx to chase off the *peltasts*.

A *peltast* carried a small shield known as a *pelta*.

An *ekdromos* didn't use a cuirass, as it would have weighed him down.

Auxiliary soldiers

Poor men who could not afford the equipment of a hoplite served in lightly armed auxiliary units. These units included archers, stone slingers and soldiers known as *psiloi*, who were armed with clubs and stones.

To protect himself, a *psilos* wore an animal skin wrapped around his arm.

The cavalry

Once hoplites came to dominate the army, the cavalry was much reduced in numbers. By the time of the Persian Wars, the Athenians had only 300 cavalry soldiers. But horsemen proved to be very useful, both as messengers and to break up an enemy phalanx. The Athenians therefore started to build up their cavalry.

Each of the ten Athenian tribes had to supply one squadron of cavalry soldiers. The cavalry was led by two commanders known as *hipparchs*, who each controlled five squadrons.

Armed with spears, javelins and swords, cavalrymen wore a metal helmet, a cuirass and boots.

Siege warfare

When one state fought with another, a common tactic was to lay siege to the enemy city. The army would surround the city and then destroy any crops growing outside the city. The enemy city would be starved into submission, but this could take a long time.

The besieging army might also take the city by force, to save time. They used a variety of weapons to attack the city walls and kill the defending soldiers. Some of these are shown below.

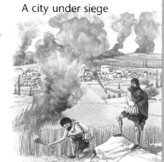
A city under siege

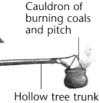
An early catapult

Javelin

The Greeks invented the catapult in the 4th century BC. Early versions were based on the crossbow and fired arrows or javelins, but later catapults could throw large rocks.

Cauldron of burning coals and pitch

Bellows

Hollow tree trunk

A flame-thrower (above) was often used to burn wooden walls. Bellows pumped air down a hollow tree trunk, spraying fire from a cauldron on to the target.

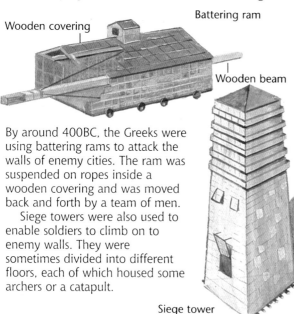
Wooden covering

Battering ram

Wooden beam

By around 400BC, the Greeks were using battering rams to attack the walls of enemy cities. The ram was suspended on ropes inside a wooden covering and was moved back and forth by a team of men.

Siege towers were also used to enable soldiers to climb on to enemy walls. They were sometimes divided into different floors, each of which housed some archers or a catapult.

Siege tower

For a link to a website where you can read about triremes and watch a short movie, go to **www.usborne-quicklinks.com**

The navy

Whereas Greek merchant ships relied on sails, fighting ships had both oars and sails. They could both be used at the same time in open sea, but sails were taken down for battle, as they slowed the ship down when turning.

The more rowers, the faster the ship went. At first, rowers sat in two lines, one on each side of the ship. Then the Phoenicians invented a ship called a *bireme*, with two rows of oars on each side of the ship, on two different levels. In the 6th century BC, the Greeks invented the *trireme*, a ship with three levels of oarsmen on each side.

The trireme

Triremes were fast and easy to turn. They probably had around 170 rowers on board. Experts think that in good sea conditions, they could reach speeds of around 16km per hour (10mph).

Triremes were unsafe in stormy seas. There was no room on board for the crew to cook or sleep, so the ship also had to land each night. But for many years, they were the most successful warships in the Mediterranean.

In Athens, the state chose a rich man to pay for the running of each ship for one year. These men, known as *trierarchs*, would often appoint professional sailors to run the ships for them.

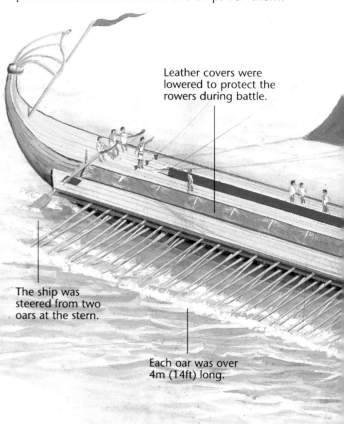
Leather covers were lowered to protect the rowers during battle.

The ship was steered from two oars at the stern.

Each oar was over 4m (14ft) long.

Early ships

In the Archaic Period, the standard Greek warship was a *penteconter*. It had 50 oarsmen. Some experts think that the oars were in one line. Others think that the oarsmen sat on two levels.

By the 8th century BC, the Phoenicians were using a warship called a *bireme*. It had two rows of oars on each side of the ship and a raised deck which carried archers and warriors.

The oarsmen

Oarsmen were professional sailors, usually recruited from the poorer classes. We do not know exactly how the three tiers of oarsmen were arranged on a trireme. Possible seating plans are shown here. Experts now think that the first arrangement is most likely.

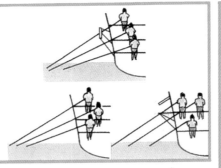

Battle tactics

At the time of the Persian Wars, trireme captains usually tried to row hard and ram the enemy ship. This would sink or at least disable it. The Greek troops then fired arrows at the enemy crew. If necessary, they boarded the enemy ship and defeated any remaining crew in hand-to-hand fighting.

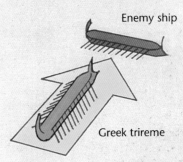

Enemy ship

Greek trireme

As triremes became swifter and lighter, tactics changed. A trireme would row toward an enemy ship, but swerve away at the last moment. The rowers pulled their oars on board and the trireme glided past the enemy ship, breaking its oars. The disabled ship could then be rammed and boarded very easily.

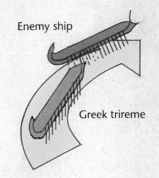

Enemy ship

Greek trireme

The mast was usually made of spruce, a wood which was imported from Thrace and Macedonia.

The sail was probably made of linen. Both the sail and mast were lowered before a battle as this made the ship easier to turn.

A trireme carried archers and soldiers who fired at the enemy and tried to board their ship.

A bronze ram attached to the front was used to sink enemy ships.

The front of the ship was often decorated with a painted eye to scare the enemy.

The Persian Wars

In the 6th century BC, the Greeks were threatened by a people known as the Persians, who came from the area that is now Iran. As the Persians expanded their empire to the west, they tried to seize Greek territory. In 546BC, they conquered the Ionian states on the west coast of Asia Minor. In 500-499BC the Ionians rebelled, helped by a naval force from Athens and Eretria. The Ionians were successful at first, but the Persians eventually crushed the revolt. This was the start of a series of wars between the Greeks and the Persians, which lasted from 490-449BC.

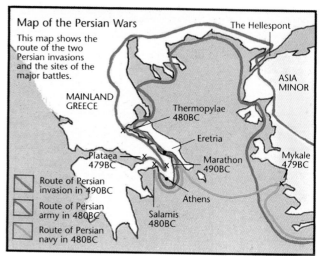

Map of the Persian Wars

This map shows the route of the two Persian invasions and the sites of the major battles.

The Hellespont

MAINLAND GREECE

ASIA MINOR

Thermopylae 480BC

Eretria

Marathon 490BC

Mykale 479BC

Plataea 479BC

Athens

Salamis 480BC

Route of Persian invasion in 490BC

Route of Persian army in 480BC

Route of Persian navy in 480BC

The Battle of Marathon

The Persians did not forgive Athens and Eretria for helping the Ionians. In 490BC, led by King Darius, they crushed Eretria. Then they landed at Marathon, on the coast northeast of Athens. The Athenians and their allies raised an army of 10,000 troops, led by a general called Miltiades. Although the Greeks were heavily outnumbered by the Persians, they won the battle. This was due to Miltiades' superior military tactics and the strength of the hoplite phalanx.

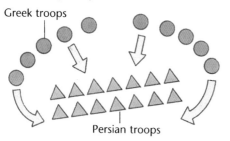

Greek troops

The Greeks concentrated their troops on the wings. They were able to attack the Persians at the sides and then from behind.

Persian troops

The second Persian invasion

Many Greeks thought the Persians would invade again. A politician called Themistocles persuaded the Athenians to increase the city's safety by building up its navy. In 480BC the Persians did invade, led by King Xerxes. Many of the Greek states joined forces to fight the Persians.

The Athenians consulted the Oracle at Delphi (see page 68) and were told that Athens would be saved by a wooden wall. Themistocles convinced the Athenians that this meant the wooden ships of the Athenian navy. He prepared for a naval battle.

In 480BC the Persians crossed the Hellespont on a bridge made of boats.

The Battle of Thermopylae

The first battle took place in 480BC in a narrow mountain pass called Thermopylae. A small army of Spartans and Boeotians, led by King Leonidas, held back the Persians. But a Greek traitor showed some of the Persians another route around the pass. Leonidas sent most of his soldiers away to safety. To delay the Persians, he fought on bravely with just a few troops, but they were all killed.

The destruction of Athens

After Thermopylae, the Persians marched to Athens. The Athenian leader Themistocles was still determined to fight the Persians at sea, so he withdrew most of his troops and allowed the Persians to seize the city. They murdered the few defending Athenians and plundered the city.

For a link to a website with more information on the Persian wars, go to www.usborne-quicklinks.com

The Battles of Salamis and Plataea

The Persians also sent a naval force to attack the Greeks. There was a decisive sea battle in 480BC around the island of Salamis, off the coast of Athens. Themistocles lured the Persians into the channel of water between Salamis and the mainland. There the Greeks took them by surprise, and after a fierce battle, the Persians were defeated.

The Battle of Salamis

In 479BC the Greeks assembled an enormous army, led by the Spartan general Pausanias, and defeated the Persians at Plataea. At the same time the Greek navy attacked and burned the Persian fleet, while it was beached at Mykale on the coast of Asia Minor. This marked the end of the Persian invasion.

The Delian League

Many Greeks believed that the Persians would try to avenge their defeat. To be ready for this, many of the Greek states formed a league, led by Athens.

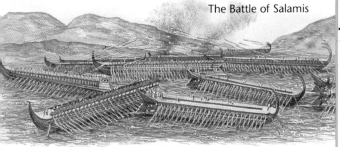

Map of the Delian League

MAINLAND GREECE

ASIA MINOR

Athens

Delos

Members of the League

Members of the league contributed ships and money to provide a navy to defend them. This is known as the Delian League, because it first met in 478BC, on Delos, one of the many Cyclades islands.

The end of the Persian Wars

Although the Greeks had stopped the Persian invasion, the wars did not come to an abrupt end. The Greeks and Persians continued to fight over various territories around the Mediterranean, such as Egypt, Cyprus and Ionia. In 449BC, the Delian League signed a peace treaty with Persia, but most Greeks continued to dislike and fear the Persians.

The Persians

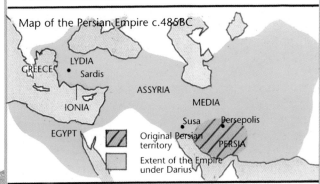

Map of the Persian Empire c.485BC

GREECE
LYDIA
Sardis
ASSYRIA
MEDIA
IONIA
Susa
Persepolis
EGYPT
PERSIA

Original Persian territory

Extent of the Empire under Darius

In 550BC, the Persians conquered the kingdom of Media and started to expand their territory, eventually acquiring a huge empire. Their empire was divided into 20 provinces. A system of roads made communication between the king and the provinces easy.

The Persians owed their success to an extremely efficient army. Most of their troops were Persian, and there was an elite force of 10,000 warriors, known as the Immortals.

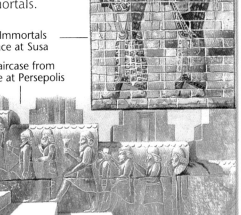

Relief of two Immortals from the palace at Susa

Part of the staircase from Darius' palace at Persepolis

Key dates

550BC King Cyrus II of Persia defeats the Medes and founds the Achaemenid dynasty.

522-485BC Reign of the Persian king, Darius I. The Persian Empire reaches its largest extent.

500-499BC The Greek colonies in Ionia revolt against the Persians, but are defeated.

490BC First Persian invasion of Greece. The Persians are defeated at the Battle of Marathon.

480BC Second Persian invasion of Greece; Battle of Thermopylae; destruction of Athens; naval Battle of Salamis.

479BC Battle of Plataea; the Greeks defeat the Persian invasion.

465-330BC Persian Empire declines and is eventually conquered by Alexander the Great (see pages 74-75).

The city of Athens

Athens is dominated by a hill called the *Acropolis*, or 'high city'. People settled there from the earliest times, because it had a spring of water and was easy to defend. In Mycenaean times there was a small city on the Acropolis, surrounded by stone walls.

By the end of the Dark Ages, the Acropolis had become a sacred place, used for temples and shrines. Other public buildings and people's houses were built around the base of the hill.

In 480BC Athens was sacked by the Persians and the temples on the Acropolis were destroyed. A few years later, the politician Pericles initiated the rebuilding of the city. The temples which still stand on the Acropolis were built at this time.

By the Classical Period, there were probably over 250,000 people living in Athens and the surrounding countryside. This reconstruction shows what the city of Athens probably looked like at the end of the Classical Period.

The Acropolis

The patron goddess of Athens was Athene, and most of the temples and shrines on the Acropolis were dedicated to her. A temple known as the *Erechtheum* was built in 421-406BC, on the site of the contest between Poseidon and Athene (see right). The temple was named after Erechtheus, the legendary ancestor of the city's Mycenaean kings.

A huge bronze statue of *Athene Promachos* (Athene the Champion) was made by the sculptor Pheidias. On clear days, it could be seen by sailors returning to the city's port at Piraeus.

The *Erechtheum*

Statue of Athene

The temple of *Athene Nike* (Athene the Victorious) was built in 426BC.

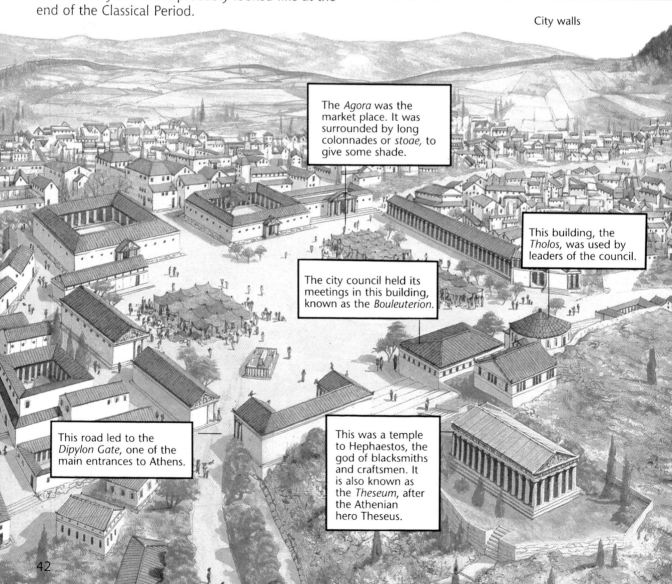

City walls

The *Agora* was the market place. It was surrounded by long colonnades or *stoae*, to give some shade.

This building, the *Tholos*, was used by leaders of the council.

The city council held its meetings in this building, known as the *Bouleuterion*.

This road led to the *Dipylon Gate*, one of the main entrances to Athens.

This was a temple to Hephaestos, the god of blacksmiths and craftsmen. It is also known as the *Theseum*, after the Athenian hero Theseus.

The *Parthenon*, another temple to the patron goddess Athene, was built between 447 and 438BC by the Greek architect Ictinus.

The *Parthenon*

Altar

This auditorium was the venue for a drama festival each year, to celebrate the god Dionysus.

Acropolis

The *Panathenaic Way* was the main road to the Acropolis. Every four years, it was used in a procession to celebrate the goddess Athene.

The Court of Justice was held on this hill, known as the *Areopagus*. It was named after the god Ares, who legends say was once tried here for murder.

Craft workers often lived in houses near the *agora*. Many blacksmiths' forges were close to the temple of Hephaestos.

The Assembly of citizens met on this hill, the *Pnyx*, to take decisions on the city's government.

The naming of Athens

According to legend, the gods Athene and Poseidon argued over the naming of the greatest town in Greece. Poseidon thrust his trident into a rock on the Acropolis. Sea water gushed out, and Poseidon promised the people riches through sea trade if they named the city after him.

Athene planted an olive tree as her gift to the people. It was decided that she had given the more valuable gift and the city was called Athens after her. Athene's sacred olive tree was burned when the city was sacked by the Persians, but when it later put out green shoots, it brought new hope to the Athenians.

The return of Theseus

Theseus was a legendary king (see page 82), said to have ruled Athens in the Mycenaean Age. At the Battle of Marathon in 490BC, the spirit of Theseus was said to have charged at the Persian ranks, inspiring the Athenians to victory.

After this the Oracle of Delphi (see page 68) ordered that Theseus' bones should be brought back to Athens from the island of Skyros, where he had died. On the island, the Athenians saw an eagle tearing at the ground. They dug in this spot and discovered a coffin containing bones and bronze weapons. They knew this must be Theseus, and reburied him in Athens.

Architecture

The Greeks attached little importance to the building of private houses, which were usually simple structures of mud and brick. Instead, they devoted their money and skills to public buildings.

The most important of these were temples, which provided a focus for civic pride and religious feelings. In the Classical Period, city-states were leading patrons for architects, sculptors and painters.

Building materials and techniques

From the 7th century BC, temples and other large, public buildings were made of stone. Masons used hammers, mallets and various kinds of chisels to shape blocks on the ground. They used ropes and pulleys to lift the blocks of stone, and then moved them into place with levers. Parts of the building, such as the roof frame and ceilings, were built from wood. Roof tiles were usually made of terracotta, although some great temples had stone tiles. This reconstructed scene shows how a temple was constructed.

A wagon carrying blocks of stone

Each block was joined to the ones beside it with pieces of metal called cramps.

Blocks were joined to the ones above and below with rods called dowels.

Cramp

Ropes and pulleys were used to lift the stone.

Masons shaping blocks of stone

Columns were made from cylindrical pieces of stone, known as drums, held together with metal pegs.

When they were in place, the stones were polished with a hard stone and a lubricant.

Grooves were marked on the pillars. This is known as fluting.

Public buildings

A reconstruction of the *tholos* in Delphi

A *tholos* was a round building with a conical roof, surrounded by columns. The *tholos* in Athens was used as a meeting place for members of the city's council.

A *stoa* was a building with a row of columns at the front. It was used to provide shelter from the sun and rain. *Stoas* were often built around an agora.

Stoas often contained stalls or offices behind the colonnade.

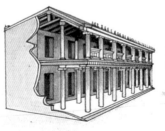

Treasuries were built at religious places to house the offerings made by a *polis* and its citizens. They consisted of a single room with a porch in front.

The Athenian treasury at Delphi

A reconstruction of the altar of Zeus and Athene at Pergamum

Altars were usually placed in the open air, usually in front of a temple entrance. They were often just a slab of stone, but some could be very large and ornate.

Architectural styles

The design of most Greek buildings was based on vertical pillars and horizontal beams, known as lintels. This style probably came from earlier buildings, where tree trunks held up the roof.

The proportions, such as the number and height of the pillars, were carefully calculated to look balanced. In the design of temples, two main styles emerged, known as the Doric and Ionic Orders.

The Doric Order

This style was popular in mainland Greece. It was a simple style with sturdy columns whose tops, or capitals, were undecorated.

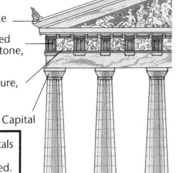

Cornice

A Doric frieze was divided up by panels of fluted stone, known as *triglyphs*.

Panels of relief sculpture, known as *metopes*, decorated the frieze.

Capital

Doric capitals were undecorated.

The Ionic Order

The Ionic style was popular in the eastern colonies and the islands. It had thinner columns than the Doric, with decorated capitals.

Pediment

Continuous frieze of sculpture

Thinner column with decorated capital and base

The swirls on the capital are called *volutes*.

Other column styles

An early form of the Ionic column has been found at Smyrna and on the island of Lesbos. This style is known as Aeolic, and may date from the 6th century BC.

The Corinthian column was a later variation of the Ionic. It had an elaborate capital, decorated with carved acanthus leaves. The Greeks did not often use Corinthian columns, but they became very popular in Roman times.

A statue of a person could also be shown. Female figures, like this, are known as *caryatids*, male figures as *atlantes* or *telamones*.

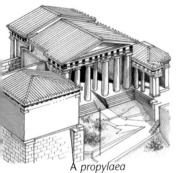

A *propylaea*

A votive monument was one set up in praise of a hero, or to celebrate a great victory in an athletic competition, a festival or a war.

A votive monument built as a war memorial

A *propylaea* was an elaborate gateway, which formed the entrance to the sacred enclosure at a religious sanctuary. The best known *propylaea* is the one on the Acropolis in Athens which was built in 437-432BC.

Decoration of buildings

The statues, friezes and sometimes also the walls of public buildings were painted. Wall paintings are often known as murals. Fragments from early murals show that a two-dimensional style was used. In the Classical Period a more lively style was introduced, and the Greeks became the first people to make use of perspective in their pictures. In the Hellenistic Period, wealthy people often had their houses decorated with murals.

Very few Greek murals have survived. However, this painting from Pompeii in Italy was probably painted by a Greek artist.

For a link to a website with pictures of ancient Greek sculptures from different periods, go to **www.usborne-quicklinks.com**

Sculpture

The Greeks made large numbers of statues. They were used to decorate homes and temples, to commemorate famous people and to mark graves. Some statues have been preserved, sometimes in unusual ways. For example, the remains of many statues have been discovered on the Acropolis in Athens, where they were buried after the city was sacked by the Persians in 480BC. Others, which were lost in shipwrecks, have been recovered from the sea. Many Roman copies of famous Greek statues have also survived although the originals have been lost.

Stone statues

Sculptors used a chisel and mallet to carve the stone.

Clothes were painted in bright shades, such as red or blue.

Hair and skin tones were also added.

Stone statues were made from limestone or marble. Blocks of stone were difficult to transport, so a rough shape was usually cut in the quarry. The detailed carving was done in a workshop, like the one shown above.

Statues were originally painted, but most of the paint has now worn away. Sometimes glass, stone or ivory was inlaid for the eyes. Details such as weapons, jewels or horses' tackle were made of bronze.

Terracotta

Terracotta is a mixture of clay and sand which was baked to make small statues and plaques for temples. It was also used to show small scenes from daily life.

A terracotta statue, from the 6th century BC, of a barber at work.

Wood

Early statues were probably made of wood, but as it decays quickly, few of them have survived. On the left is a rare wooden statue of Zeus and Hera, made in c.625-600BC.

Bronze

The Greeks also made many bronze statues, but only a few of them have survived. Some of these are shown on page 48.

Styles of sculpture

The Archaic Period: c.800-480BC

At first statues were only made in a limited number of poses, which were copied from Egyptian art. Normally the figure was standing in a very stiff, formal position, with its left leg forward and arms at its sides. Its facial expression was always in a half-smile.

The Classical Period: c.480-323BC

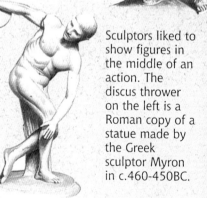

In this period, it was fashionable for sculptors to portray deities, or god-like men and women, with calm and serene facial expressions. The statue on the right is a Roman copy of figure by Praxiteles, c.350-330BC.

Sculptors liked to show figures in the middle of an action. The discus thrower on the left is a Roman copy of a statue made by the Greek sculptor Myron in c.460-450BC.

The Hellenistic Period: c.323-100BC

Egyptian statue   Greek statues

Greek artists gradually became dissatisfied with this formal approach and began experimenting with relaxed and supple figures and more adventurous poses. The statue below of an archer was made c.500-480BC.

Sculptors also started to show the folds of material in clothes. At first these were just rigid lines, but they became more flowing, as shown on this figure of a goddess, made in c.480BC.

As sculptors became more skilled at showing facial expressions, they began to produce portraits. On the right is the Athenian leader Pericles (see page 62).

Sculptors also made reliefs – figures carved on slabs of stone. They were often used to decorate temple walls. The scene below from the Parthenon shows riders in the *Panathenaic* procession (see page 67).

Athens was famous for carving gravestones. The gravestone below, for a woman named Hegeso, was made in c.400BC.

There was also a growing interest in portraying the female body. The first known female nude is the statue on the left of Aphrodite by Praxiteles, made c.350-330BC.

Sculptors also made special reliefs which people left in temples to thank the gods. The one on the left was dedicated to Asclepius, the god of medicine.

In the 4th century BC, sculptors became more interested in human emotions. Facial expressions on statues were often gentle and tender. The Roman copy on the right shows the mythical characters Eirene and Ploutos.

In the Hellenistic Period, sculptors started to portray a wider range of characters. Old age, childhood, pain and even death were now acceptable subjects. On the left is a Roman copy of a statue showing a dying man.

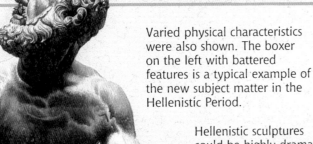

Varied physical characteristics were also shown. The boxer on the left with battered features is a typical example of the new subject matter in the Hellenistic Period.

Hellenistic sculptures could be highly dramatic. The statue on the right shows a man killing himself and his wife.

Metalworkers and miners

In the Mycenaean period, most weapons and tools were made from bronze. Iron was introduced in the Dark Ages, but it was only used for some objects. Gold and silver were used for luxury items.

In Athens, the metalworkers had their own quarter near the temple of Hephaestos, who was their patron deity. Most smiths worked in small workshops in their homes.

Bronze

Bronze is made by adding a small amount of tin to copper. The Greeks imported copper from Cyprus and the eastern Mediterranean and tin from Spain, Brittany in France and even Cornwall in England. They used bronze to make a wide variety of objects, some of which are shown here. As bronze was a valuable metal, it was often melted down and reused, so few large items have survived.

Bronze was the preferred material for statues. Some of the statues we have were originally lost at sea in shipwrecks and have only recently been found by underwater archaeologists.

This statue probably represents the god Poseidon throwing a trident. It was made in c.470-450BC.

Portrait head of a North African man, made in c.350BC

This statue of a jockey and his horse was probably a victory monument from the Olympic Games.

Weapons and other war gear were usually made of bronze. This vase painting shows a helmet being made.

Bronze was used for household objects, such as vases, mirrors and kitchen utensils. This bronze mirror was made in c.500BC.

This enormous bronze *krater* was discovered at Vix in France. It is 1.64m (5.4ft) high.

Methods of working bronze

Hammering

Early bronze statues were made from sheets of bronze hammered over a wooden core.

Casting

Later, metal was melted and then cast to make small, solid statues.

The lost wax method

Not all cast statues were solid metal. Some were made by the lost wax method, shown below. Large statues were made in sections and joined together.

Clay core

Wax model built around core

1. A clay core was made, with pins for support. The statue was shaped around the core in wax.

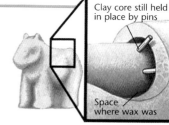

Clay core still held in place by pins

Space where wax was

2. The model was covered in clay and heated. The wax melted and ran out, leaving a space.

Finished statue

3. Molten bronze was poured into the gap. When the bronze had set, the clay was removed.

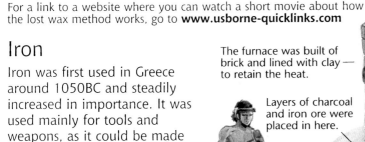

For a link to a website where you can watch a short movie about how the lost wax method works, go to **www.usborne-quicklinks.com**

Iron

Iron was first used in Greece around 1050BC and steadily increased in importance. It was used mainly for tools and weapons, as it could be made sharper and harder than bronze.

Ironworking required some clever new technology. The furnace needed to be heated to a much higher temperature than for bronze.

This reconstruction of an iron furnace is based on one shown on a vase painting. When the furnace was heated, the molten iron gathered at the bottom and could be removed with tongs.

The furnace was built of brick and lined with clay — to retain the heat.

Layers of charcoal and iron ore were placed in here.

One man pumped goatskin bellows to make the fire burn hotter in the furnace.

Iron had to be hammered while it was still red hot, to remove impurities.

Special tongs were used to move the hot metal.

This golden casket was found in the royal Macedonian tombs in Vergina.

A silver jug from the Macedonian tombs

A gold bowl from Olympia, c.620BC

Gold and silver

Precious metals were used to make coins, jewels and luxury goods. We also know of several large statues made of gold and ivory, such as the statue of Athene in the Parthenon (see page 66). Not many ancient Greek gold and silver objects have survived, as they were often melted down so that the metal could be reused. When the Romans occupied Greece in the 2nd century BC, they stole huge numbers of gold and silver objects. Tomb-robbers have also stolen a lot over the years.

Silver mining

Most of the Greeks' silver came from mines at Laurion, near Athens. These mines were worked from at least the 8th century BC.

The mines were owned by the Athenian state, but they were leased out to private contractors. The mining itself was done by slaves, who were hired from their owners. Conditions were grim, with miners working shifts of up to ten hours. This reconstruction of a mine shows how ore was extracted.

Narrow galleries fanned out into the seams of silver ore. In some places miners had to crawl along them and then lie on their backs to work.

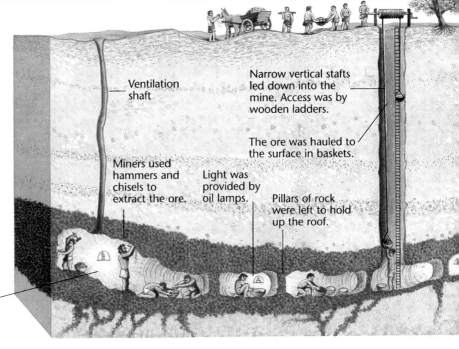

Ventilation shaft

Narrow vertical stafts led down into the mine. Access was by wooden ladders.

The ore was hauled to the surface in baskets.

Miners used hammers and chisels to extract the ore.

Light was provided by oil lamps.

Pillars of rock were left to hold up the roof.

The role of women

Women in most states in ancient Greece led very sheltered lives and were not allowed to play an active role in society. They couldn't inherit or own property, or bring cases in the law courts.

They could not even buy anything that cost over a certain amount of money. They were always under the control of a male relative: first their father, then their husband, brother or son.

Marriage

A girl was around 15 when she was married, but the bridegroom was older. One writer thought that 30-35 was the best age for a man to marry.

A girl's father chose her husband and gave her money and goods, known as a dowry. This returned to her father if her husband divorced her, or died.

Loutrophorus

Servants dressing the bride

On the day before her wedding a bride bathed in water from a sacred spring, brought in a special vase called a *loutrophorus*.

On the wedding day, the bride wore white. Both families made sacrifices and feasted. In the evening, the groom went to the bride's house.

The bride and groom then rode to his house in a cart, or in a chariot if they were rich. Torchbearers and musicians led the procession.

The groom's mother met the procession. The bride was then led to the hearth, to join the religious life of her new family.

The bride and groom shared some food before the hearth. The guests showered them with nuts, fruits and sweets for luck and prosperity.

The next day a party was held at the husband's house, and guests gave presents to the couple, as they began their new lives together.

A wife's duties

In a wealthy household, a bride had many duties. She inspected the stores and ensured that the house was clean and that meals were ready on time. She looked after the children and any sick members of the household, and managed the family finances.

The women of the household produced all the cloth needed for clothes and furnishings. This reconstruction, based on a 6th century vase painting, shows a wife supervising the various stages involved in making cloth.

The mistress of the household is preparing some wool for spinning, and supervising the work.

This woman is spinning the wool. She holds the wool on a distaff and uses a spindle to twist and stretch the thread.

The thread is woven into cloth on a loom.

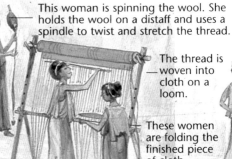

These women are weighing wads of wool on a pair of scales.

These women are folding the finished piece of cloth.

For a link to a website where you can find more wedding facts and pictures, go to **www.usborne-quicklinks.com**

Social life

The slave carried a parasol to protect his mistress from the Sun.

In Athens, married women from wealthy families didn't often leave the house. They only went out for religious festivals and family celebrations, or to do small bits of personal shopping. When they did go out, a slave accompanied them.

Sometimes they were allowed to visit their women friends. This terracotta statue shows two ladies chatting. Women also gave dinner parties for their female friends. Men and women only mixed at strictly family parties.

Generally, the richer the family, the less freedom the wife had. In poor families, the women did the housework themselves. This involved going shoppping and fetching water from the fountain, which were both good opportunities to meet friends.

Divorce

Though men could do more or less as they liked, women had to behave according to strict rules: at any suspicion of scandal, they might face divorce.

To divorce his wife, a man just made a formal statement of divorce in front of witnesses. It was much more difficult for a woman to end her marriage, as she could not take legal action herself. She had to go to an official called an *archon* (see page 61) and persuade him to act on her behalf.

In a divorce, the husband kept the children and sent his wife back to her nearest male relative.

Hetairai

Hetairai could join men's dinner parties. They were trained to join in the conversation.

Some girls, usually from the lower classes or foreigners, would become *hetairai*, or companions. They had to be pretty and clever, and were carefully trained to be skilled musicians and witty, interesting speakers. They took wealthy lovers who could support them in comfort.

Beauty

Oil bottles in the shape of feet

Ladies spent a lot of time, effort and money on making themselves beautiful. It became the custom to have a bath every day. After the bath, perfumed oil was rubbed into the skin to moisturize it and to keep it smooth and supple.

This vase painting shows a woman washing her hair. Oil was also used to make the hair shine. Some women dyed their hair or used wigs. Others used padding to improve their figure, or wore thick-soled sandals to make themselves taller.

Many women used rouge to make their cheeks pink, and darkened their eyebrows. Pale skin was fashionable and makeup was used to make the skin look white. This vase painting shows a woman admiring herself in a mirror.

Childhood and education

Greek people were encouraged to have sons to provide citizens and soldiers. Parents also benefited from having a son, as it ensured there would be someone to support them in their old age.

Daughters could not support their parents because they were not allowed to inherit property or money. If a man did not have a son, he could adopt a boy who would inherit from him.

Babies

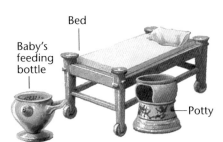

Bed

Baby's feeding bottle

Potty

When a baby was born, the mother presented it to her husband. If he did not believe that it was his child, or if the baby was not in perfect health, he could reject it. The baby would then be left to die.

People who didn't want another child might also abandon their babies. In some states unwanted babies were left in a specific place. People could go there and adopt a child to be their slave.

Rich families would hire a poor person or a slave as a nurse for the baby. They also had special furniture made for their children, some of which has been found on the sites of excavated houses.

Seven days after the birth of a baby, the front door of the house was decorated with garlands of olive leaves for a boy or wool for a girl. The family made a sacrifice to the gods and held a party.

A ceremony called the *amphidromia* took place at the party. The women of the house carried the baby around the hearth to bring it into the religious life of the family. The baby was usually named as well.

At the age of three, a child's infancy was thought to be over. In Athens this was marked at the *Anthesteria* festival (see page 67). On the second day of the festival, three-year-olds were given small jugs like this one.

Education in Sparta

The state of Sparta was very worried about being attacked, so its education was all about toughness and physical fitness. The most important subjects were athletics, dancing and weapon training. Some music, Spartan law and poetry were also taught, although they were not considered very important. The Spartans aimed to produce tough, healthy adults to become warriors and mothers of warriors.

At seven, a boy was sent to live in a barracks, supervised by a teacher known as a *paidonome*.

Each boy belonged to a group, and several groups made up a class. Group leaders organized the work.

Boys had to make their own beds from rushes. They weren't allowed to have covers.

From the age of 12, boys went bareheaded and barefooted.

For a link to a website where you can find out more about education in ancient Greece, go to **www.usborne-quicklinks.com**

School

A boy's education usually began at the age of seven, and could go on until he started his military training at 18 (see page 36). In Greek education, physical fitness was considered to be as important as learning.

As education had to be paid for, it is unlikely that poor children received more than a basic schooling. Girls were usually taught by their mothers at home. A rich family often hired a slave known as a *paidagogos* to supervize their son's schooling.

Grammatistes — Wax covered tablet

Paidagogos

Poems were written on scrolls of papyrus.

A boy attended three schools. The first was run by a teacher known as a *grammatistes*, who taught reading, writing and arithmetic. Pupils wrote with a stylus on wooden tablets covered in wax.

A boy was taught music and poetry by a *kitharistes*. He also learned to play the lyre and the pipes. He had to learn poetry by heart, as an educated man was expected to quote poetry in his conversation.

The third type of school was run by a *paidotribes*, who taught dancing and athletics. He probably took his pupils to a *gymnasium* (a training ground) or a *palaistra* (a wrestling school) to train.

Higher education

There was no formal higher education, but from the 5th century BC, teachers called *sophists* went from place to place instructing young men in the art of public speaking. Philosophers like Socrates often taught informally at a *gymnasium* and attracted groups of devoted young followers. In the 4th century BC, Plato, Aristotle and others set up permanent schools at *gymnasia* in Athens. By the Hellenistic Period, it was common for *gymnasia* to provide lecture rooms and libraries as part of their facilities.

Philosophers taught under the colonnades or in the dressing rooms at a *gymnasium*. They discussed subjects such as mathematics, science, politics and history.

The food was inadequate and the boys were encouraged to steal extra food from the local farms, to make them cunning.

Each year there was a competition in which the boys were beaten to see who could bear the most pain. Some boys died during the thrashing.

Boys bathed in the river.

Boys were allowed to attend the men's meals in the barracks. They listened and took part in the discussions, but absolute respect and obedience to their elders was expected.

A Spartan dancing class

Spartan girls were also educated in order to produce physically fit and disciplined women. They were trained in gymnastics, music, singing and dancing, and took part in athletic competitions.

Music and poetry

Music was very important in the daily lives of most Greeks. There was music for many social events: songs to celebrate a birth or lament a death, drinking songs and love songs. There were work songs for farmers, and warriors and athletes trained to the sound of pipe music. Music was also used to accompany poetry, religious festivals and theatrical performances (see page 56).

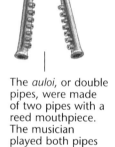

The sons and daughters of citizens were usually taught music. This vase painting shows a child being taught to play the double pipes, known as *auloi*.

Musical instruments

We do not know what Greek music sounded like because it wasn't usually written down. Only some fragments of pieces of music have been found and it is difficult to interpret what the symbols mean.

We do know what Greek musical instruments looked like, however, because they were often depicted on vases and in paintings. Some popular instruments are shown here.

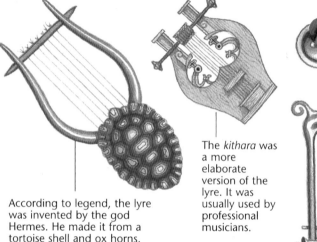

According to legend, the lyre was invented by the god Hermes. He made it from a tortoise shell and ox horns.

The *kithara* was a more elaborate version of the lyre. It was usually used by professional musicians.

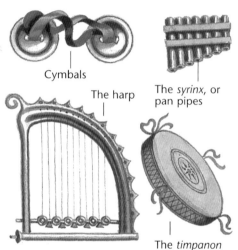

Cymbals

The harp

The *syrinx*, or pan pipes

The *timpanon*

The *auloi*, or double pipes, were made of two pipes with a reed mouthpiece. The musician played both pipes at the same time.

Poetry

In Greece, music and poetry were closely linked. Poetry was usually performed in public, rather than read privately. The words were sung or chanted, often with a musical accompaniment.

Men known as *rhapsodes* made their living by reciting poetry at religious festivals or at private parties. They knew long epic poems such as Homer's *Odyssey* and *Iliad* (see page 17) by heart.

This vase painting shows a *rhapsode* reciting from a podium.

Apollo and the Muses

Apollo was the god of music and poetry, and is often shown with a lyre or a *kithara*. According to legend, the lyre was invented by Apollo's half-brother Hermes, who gave the instrument to Apollo in exchange for some cattle which he had stolen from him.

Apollo is closely associated with nine goddesses known as the Muses, who were believed to inspire and guide people's creative and intellectual activities. Each of them was responsible for a particular art, such as poetry, music or dance.

For a link to a website where you can listen to modern interpretations of ancient Greek music, go to **www.usborne-quicklinks.com**

Parties

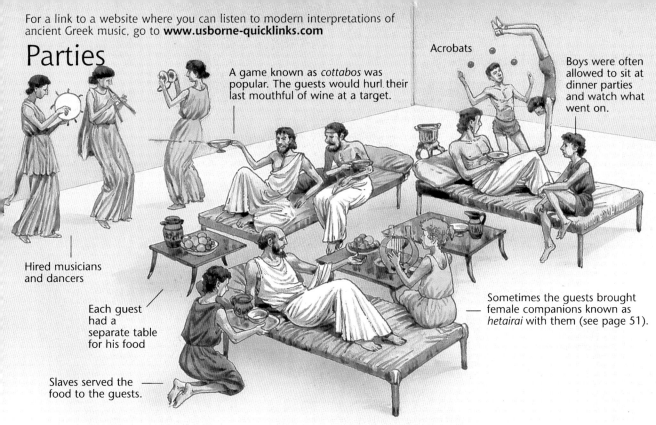

A game known as *cottabos* was popular. The guests would hurl their last mouthful of wine at a target.

Acrobats

Boys were often allowed to sit at dinner parties and watch what went on.

Hired musicians and dancers

Each guest had a separate table for his food

Slaves served the food to the guests.

Sometimes the guests brought female companions known as *hetairai* with them (see page 51).

Dinner parties were a popular leisure activity. A man would invite several male friends to his house for a meal. The guests were met at the door by slaves who washed their hands and feet. Then they lay on couches in a room known as the *andron*, where food was served by slaves. Once the food was cleared away, the drinking and talking began.

This was known as a *symposium*. The guests drank wine which had been mixed with water in a vase known as a *krater*. The conversation might be about morals or politics, but often parties were relaxed, with guests playing the lyre, reciting poetry or telling jokes. Additional entertainment might be provided by hired musicians, dancers or acrobats.

Toys and games

Animal fighting was considered a sport. Cocks, quails, or a cat and dog would fight to the death.

This vase painting shows two warriors playing a board game, which may have been like chess.

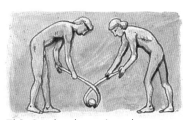

The Greeks also enjoyed sport. This carving shows a game which looks rather like modern hockey.

Adults often played dice, either at home or in special gaming houses. Another popular game, which we know as knucklebones or jacks, involved throwing small bones.

Baby's rattle

Spinning top

Doll

Wealthy families gave their children many games and toys to amuse them in their leisure hours.

Yo-yo

Some of them are shown here.

Hoop and stick

For a link to a website where you can go on an interactive trip to see ancient Greek drama, go to **www.usborne-quicklinks.com**

Plays and players

The origins of drama in the western world can be traced back to ancient Greece. It developed from a countryside festival, held in praise of the god Dionysus. In Athens, this developed into an annual event, known as the *City Dionysia*. Songs were specially composed each year and were performed along with dances by a group of men known as a *chorus*. There were prizes for the best entry.

At first, the chorus performed in the market place, but later a huge open-air auditorium was built on the slopes of the Acropolis. Later, similar structures were built all over the Greek world. Most of them could hold at least 18,000 spectators.

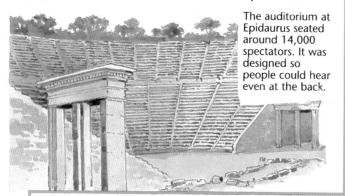

The auditorium at Epidaurus seated around 14,000 spectators. It was designed so people could hear even at the back.

At a performance

The reconstruced scene on the right shows how a play might have looked in progress. Important people, such as leading citizens, foreign visitors or competition judges, sat at the front of the auditorium.

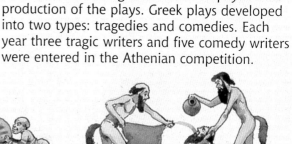

Important people sat on special stone seats like this one.

Tokens like the ones on the left were used as tickets. The letters on them show which block the ticket holder could sit in. Seats cost two obols. From the time of Pericles, the state paid for poor people's tickets.

Tokens

The Athens drama festival

In Athens, the *Dionysia* was one of the city's most important religious celebrations. The festival, which lasted for five days, was a public holiday so that everyone could attend. The first day was devoted to processions and sacrifices. The remaining four days were taken up with drama competitions.

The *Dionysia* was organized by an *archon* (see page 61). He picked a number of rich citizens, known as the *choregoi*, who had to pay for the production of the plays. Greek plays developed into two types: tragedies and comedies. Each year three tragic writers and five comedy writers were entered in the Athenian competition.

Scene from a tragedy

Scene from a comedy

Scene from a *satyr* play

Tragedies were usually written about the heroes of the past. They concentrated on grand themes such as whether to obey or defy the will of the gods, human passions and conflicts or the misuse of power. The best known tragic writers are Aeschylus, Sophocles and Euripides.

In comedy, characters were usually ordinary people. The dialogue often included comments on the politics and personalities of the day, along with clowning, slapstick comedy and rude jokes. The best known ancient Greek comic writer is Aristophanes. His plays include *The Birds* and *The Frogs*.

In the comedy competition each author entered one play. But in the tragedy section, each writer had to enter three tragedies and a *satyr* play. This was a play which made fun of the tragic theme. The chorus dressed as *satyrs* – wild followers of Dionysus who were half man and half beast.

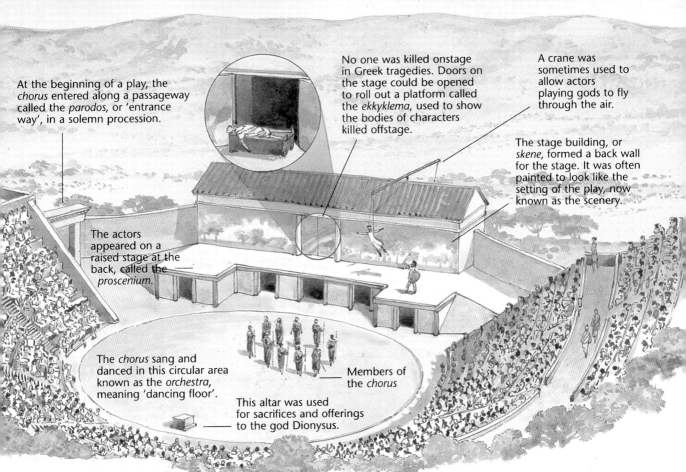

At the beginning of a play, the *chorus* entered along a passageway called the *parodos,* or 'entrance way', in a solemn procession.

No one was killed onstage in Greek tragedies. Doors on the stage could be opened to roll out a platform called the *ekkyklema,* used to show the bodies of characters killed offstage.

A crane was sometimes used to allow actors playing gods to fly through the air.

The stage building, or *skene,* formed a back wall for the stage. It was often painted to look like the setting of the play, now known as the scenery.

The actors appeared on a raised stage at the back, called the *proscenium.*

The *chorus* sang and danced in this circular area known as the *orchestra,* meaning 'dancing floor'.

Members of the *chorus*

This altar was used for sacrifices and offerings to the god Dionysus.

The performers

All the performers in Greek plays were men. At first, plays consisted simply of the chorus singing and dancing, but later an actor was introduced to exchange dialogue with the leader of the *chorus.*

A second and third actor were later added, and they often played several roles each. The dialogue between the actors eventually became the most important part of the drama.

Costumes

Chorus member dressed as a bird

Male actor dressed as a woman

Comic actors

Happy characters wore bright costumes, and tragic ones dark costumes. Because of the size of theatres, actors had to be visible and clothes were often padded to give them bulk. They wore large wigs and thick-soled shoes to look taller. In comedies, the *chorus* also wore costumes and sometimes even dressed as birds or animals.

Masks

Each actor wore a painted mask made of stiffened fabric or cork. The expression on the mask showed the character's age, sex and feelings. Actors could change parts quickly simply by swapping masks. The expressions on the masks were easily visible, even from the back of the theatre.

Athletics and sports

One of the most popular pastimes for Greek men was athletics. The Greek states encouraged their citizens to take part in sports, because this kept them fit and meant that they would be in good condition for fighting, if a war began.

The Olympic Games

The Olympic Games were the most important of the competitions. They probably developed from funeral games held in memory of the hero Pelops (see page 83). They started in 776BC and were held every four years at Olympia, in praise of Zeus.

Before the Games, messengers journeyed through Greece and the colonies, announcing the date of the Games and inviting people to attend.

There were many competitions which athletes could enter. Most were only local affairs, but four events (the Olympic, Pythian, Isthmian and Nemean Games) attracted athletes from all over the Greek world. They were known as the Panhellenic Games.

All wars had to cease until the Games were over, to allow people to travel to Olympia in safety.

At Olympia, a group of impressive buildings were built for the Games. These included sports grounds for the various events, facilities for the competitors and spectators, and temples for the religious ceremonies. This is a reconstruction of how Olympia would have looked at its largest.

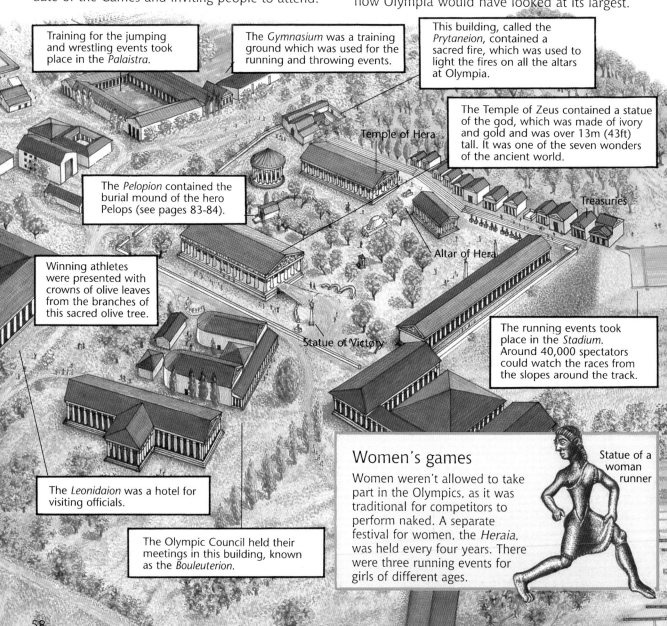

Training for the jumping and wrestling events took place in the *Palaistra*.

The *Gymnasium* was a training ground which was used for the running and throwing events.

This building, called the *Prytaneion*, contained a sacred fire, which was used to light the fires on all the altars at Olympia.

Temple of Hera

The Temple of Zeus contained a statue of the god, which was made of ivory and gold and was over 13m (43ft) tall. It was one of the seven wonders of the ancient world.

The *Pelopion* contained the burial mound of the hero Pelops (see pages 83-84).

Treasuries

Altar of Hera

Winning athletes were presented with crowns of olive leaves from the branches of this sacred olive tree.

Statue of Victory

The running events took place in the *Stadium*. Around 40,000 spectators could watch the races from the slopes around the track.

The *Leonidaion* was a hotel for visiting officials.

Women's games

Women weren't allowed to take part in the Olympics, as it was traditional for competitors to perform naked. A separate festival for women, the *Heraia*, was held every four years. There were three running events for girls of different ages.

Statue of a woman runner

The Olympic Council held their meetings in this building, known as the *Bouleuterion*.

For a link to a website where you can take a virt ancient Olympic games, go to **www.usborne-c**

Running

A vase painting of a race in which athletes wore helmets and carried shields

The running track in the *Stadium* was around 192m (640ft) long and was made of clay covered with sand. There were three main races: the *stade* (one length of the track), the *diaulos* (two lengths) and the *dolichos* (20 or 24 lengths).

Wrestling

There were three wrestling events. In upright wrestling, an athlete had to throw his opponent three times to win. In ground wrestling, the contest went on until one man gave in. In the *pankration*, any tactic except biting and eye-gouging was permitted.

The pentathlor

A vase painting of a jumper, a discus thrower and two javelin throwers

The *pentathlon* was a competition consisting of five athletic events: running, wrestling, jumping, discus and javelin throwing. It was a very demanding competition, which required great strength and endurance.

Boxing

At first, the contestants' hands were bound with leather thongs. Later, special boxing gloves were developed.

A boxing contest could go on for hours and was only decided when one athlete lost consciousness or conceded defeat. Athletes therefore aimed most of their punches at their opponents' heads. Virtually any blow with the hand was permitted.

Chariot races

There were chariot races for teams of two or four horses. The course consisted of 12 laps around two posts in the ground. At the start, the chariots were released from a special starting gate. As many as 40 chariots could take part in one race.

Horse races

The basic horse race was run over a distance of around 1200m (4000ft). In another race the rider dismounted and ran the last stretch beside his horse. Jockeys rode bareback and accidents were very common.

The winners

Winners were presented with palm branches, a wreath of olive leaves, and wool ribbons.

Prizes were given on the fifth day of the games. It was thought that athletes should seek only the privilege of competing and the personal glory of winning. However, a winning athlete could reap many material rewards. By the 5th century BC, some athletes were professionals, making their living by representing the city states at various games. A city gained prestige by sponsoring a successful athlete, and would pay him well.

The modern Olympics

The ancient Olympics ended in AD395, when Olympia was destroyed by two earthquakes. In AD1896 a French athlete, named le Baron Pierre de Coubertin, was inspired by the ideals of the competition and organized the first modern Olympics. Many aspects of the ancient games have been preserved. For example the modern ceremony of lighting the Olympic Flame is based on an ancient type of relay race, in which a torch was passed from one runner to the next. The last runner of the winning team lit a fire on an altar.

Democracy in Athens

At the end of the Archaic Period, some Greek states overthrew their tyrants and adopted a system of government known as *democracy*. The name comes from the Greek words *demos* (people) and *kratos* (rule). Under this system, all full citizens were allowed to have a say in the government of their city-state.

These pages describe how democracy worked in Athens. It was first introduced there in 508BC by the leader Cleisthenes. Today, the term democracy is used to describe a system in which everybody has a vote. In ancient Greece, only citizens had this right. All other social groups, such as women, foreign residents and slaves, were excluded.

Local organization

Cleisthenes split the people of Attica (Athens and the surrounding area) into different groups for administrative purposes.

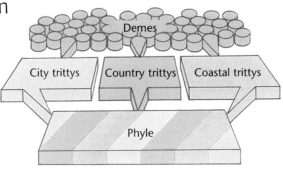

Attica was divided into small communities known as *demes*. *Demes* were put into 30 larger groups, or *trittyes*. Ten *trittyes* represented the city of Athens, ten the countryside and ten the coastal areas. *Trittyes* were grouped into ten *phylai*, or tribes. Each *phyle* was made up of three *trittyes*: one from the city, one from the country and one from the coast.

The Assembly

Each citizen had the right to speak and to vote at the Assembly, which met around once every ten days on a hill called the Pnyx. At least 6,000 citizens had to be present for a meeting to take place. The Assembly debated proposals which were put to it by the Council (see right). It could approve, change or reject the Council's suggestions.

An Assembly meeting on the Pnyx

The Council

The 50 councillors on duty met in this building, known as the *Tholos*. It was staffed day and night, in case of emergency.

The Council drew up new laws and policies, which were then debated in the Assembly. The Council was made up of 500 citizens, 50 from each of the 10 Athenian tribes. Each tribal group took turns to lead the Council, taking responsibility for the day-to-day running of the state.

The legal system

One of a citizen's duties was to participate in the running of the legal system. All citizens over 30 were expected to volunteer for jury service. From 461BC jurors were paid, to compensate them for any loss of earnings. There were no professional judges, lawyers or legal officials. Each court had a jury of over 200 men, so there were far too many to be bribed or intimidated.

As there were no lawyers, citizens conducted their own cases. Some employed speech writers to prepare their cases for them. Only citizens could speak in court. If a *metic* was accused, he had to persuade a citizen to speak on his behalf.

Often more people volunteered for jury service than were needed. This machine, known as a *kleroterion*, was used to select the names of the jurors for that day automatically.

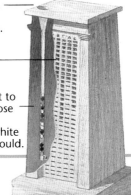

White and black balls were dropped in here.

Jurors' names rested in these slots.

A black ball next to a row meant those men would not serve today, a white one that they would.

The archons

In the Archaic Period, the most important officials were *archons* (see page 21). Under democracy, a lot of their power went to the *strategoi* (see below).

There were nine *archons*, chosen ã from the citizens. Three of them wei important than the others and had specia.

The *Basileus Archon* presided over the *Areopagus* or Court of Justice, arranged religious sacrifices, and organized the renting of temple land. He also supervised the drama festival and other feasts.

The *Eponymous Archon* chose the men who were to finance the choral and drama contests. He was also responsible for lawsuits about inheritances and the affairs of heiresses, orphans and widows.

The *Polemarch Archon* was in charge of offerings and special athletic contests held as tributes to men killed in war. He also dealt with the legal affairs of *metics* (foreign residents of Athens).

The strategoi

When Athens sent an army or navy into battle, it was led by one or two *strategoi*.

The *strategoi* were military commanders (see page 36) who also had the power to implement the policies decided by the Council and the Assembly. There were ten *strategoi*, one from each of the Athenian tribes. They were elected annually and could be re-elected many times. The *strategoi* had to answer to the Assembly for their actions.

Ostracism

These *ostraka* show the names of two politicians, named Aristides and Cimon.

Ostracism was a system used to remove unpopular politicians. A vote of ostracism could be held once a year in the Assembly. Each citizen wrote the name of any politician he wished to see banished on a piece of broken pottery, known as an *ostrakon*. If a politician received more than 6000 votes, he had to leave Athens for 10 years.

Each juror was issued with two different bronze tokens, which were used for voting. At the end of the trial, he handed in one of them to show whether he thought the accused person was innocent or guilty.

The token with a solid bar in the middle meant 'innocent'.

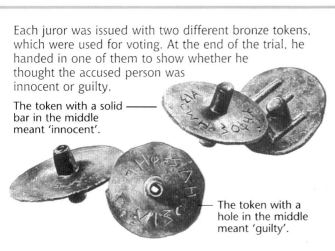

The token with a hole in the middle meant 'guilty'.

Certain jurors, who were chosen by lot, were given special tasks. One took charge as the judge, four counted the votes and one worked a water clock like the one shown here. This was used to limit the time allowed to each speaker.

The upper pot was filled with water.

When all the water had run through into this lower pot, the speaker's time was up.

The Golden Age and the Peloponnesian War

The Persian Wars were followed by an era of great prosperity and achievement in Athens. This is known as its Golden Age (479-431BC). Trade flourished and the city became very rich. Athens became a leading city for the arts, attracting the best sculptors, potters, architects, dramatists and philosophers. This security was shattered by the Peloponnesian War between Athens and Sparta. It lasted for 27 years (431-404BC) and left the city-states weak and exhausted. Athens never regained its former power.

During the Golden Age, the city was improved and the temples on the Acropolis were rebuilt.

Pericles

The democratic system was finalized during this time. The most famous politician was Pericles, who dominated Athenian politics from 443-429BC, as he was elected repeatedly. He was a powerful public speaker and usually persuaded the Assembly to vote the way he wanted. One of his most notable achievements was to organize the rebuilding of the Acropolis.

Bust of Pericles

Relations between Sparta and Athens

Soon after the Persian Wars, relations between Sparta and Athens began to deteriorate. As Athens grew powerful and wealthy, the Spartans felt threatened.

In c.460BC the *helots* and the people of Messenia rebelled against Sparta. The Spartans asked Athens for help, but by the time the Athenians arrived, the Spartans had changed their minds. They were so distrustful of democrats that they would not let the Athenians intervene. The Athenians felt bitterly insulted and abandoned their alliance with Sparta.

The Long Walls

In 460BC, the Athenians began building huge walls linking their city to its port at Piraeus. They are known as the Long Walls. They meant that Athens could not be cut off from the its navy. The Spartans thought this meant that Athens was preparing for war, and fighting broke out between the two states in 448-447BC.

After this, Sparta and Athens signed a treaty known as the Thirty Years' Peace, but relations between them remained hostile.

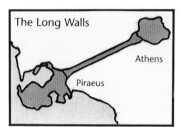

The Long Walls

Athens

Piraeus

The Peloponnesian War begins

In 431BC, hostilities broke out between Corinth and its colony of Corcyra (modern Corfu). Sparta supported Corinth and Athens backed Corcyra. This began the Peloponnesian War. It was given this name because Sparta was supported by a league of states in the Peloponnese, which is the southern part of mainland Greece. Athens was backed by its allies in the Delian League.

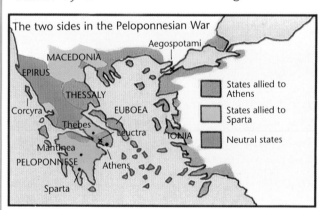

The two sides in the Peloponnesian War

Aegospotami

MACEDONIA

EPIRUS

THESSALY

Corcyra

EUBOEA

Thebes

Leuctra

IONIA

Mantinea

PELOPONNESE

Athens

Sparta

States allied to Athens

States allied to Sparta

Neutral states

The Spartans were nearly unbeatable in land battles. They were easily able to invade Attica. The Athenians had a superior navy and a weaker army than the Spartans. They tried to avoid fighting the Spartans on land. They stayed inside their city walls and imported food by sea. This resulted in a long deadlock.

The Spartans devastated the countryside around Athens, but could not get through the Long Walls.

The Sicilian expedition

In 430BC, a plague broke out in Athens, in which around a quarter of the people died. By 421BC both sides were exhausted and signed a treaty.

But war broke out again and events soon turned against Athens. In 415BC a politician called Alcibiades persuaded the Athenians to attack Syracuse, in Sicily. Before the attack, he was told to return to Athens to face charges brought against him by his enemies. Instead, he fled to Sparta and advised the Spartans on how to defeat Athens. The Athenians were defeated at Syracuse and many of their troops were massacred.

Around 7000 of the surviving Athenians were forced to work in stone quarries on Sicily.

Political unrest in Athens

In 411BC a council of 400 men seized power in Athens and abolished democracy. The news caused Athenian forces overseas to mutiny. After three months, democracy was restored. The Athenians needed a strong leader, so they recalled Alcibiades and made him *strategos*. But he failed to fulfil their hopes and was not re-elected. Support for the Athenians declined and some of their allies withdrew from the Delian League.

The Spartans build a fleet

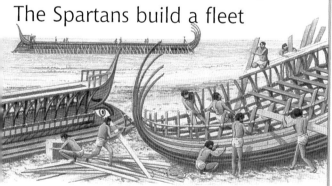

Meanwhile the Persians intervened. They were fighting the Greek colonists in Ionia, who were supported by the Spartans. The Persians persuaded the Spartans to withdraw from Ionia by giving them money to build a fleet. This enabled the Spartans to attack the Athenians at sea as well as on land.

The Battle of Aegospotami

In 405BC, the Spartans scored a decisive naval victory. They launched a surprise attack on the Athenian fleet when it was docked at Aegospotami in Thrace. The Spartans captured 170 Athenian ships and executed around 4000 prisoners. It was a blow from which Athens never recovered.

The Athenians had gone ashore at Aegospotami to eat when the Spartans attacked.

The Spartans then laid siege to Athens. Without a fleet, the Athenians were unable to import food, and many people starved. In 404BC, they had to surrender. The Spartans pulled down the Long Walls, ended the Delian League and abolished democracy. They installed an oligarchic government known as the Thirty Tyrants.

After the Peloponnesian War

The Spartans' victory did not bring peace or unity to Greece. They began to lose control in Athens, where democracy was restored in 403BC. Wars broke out again between the various states. Most Greeks were too absorbed in these problems to notice a new power rising in Macedonia, to the northeast. The Macedonians began expanding their territory, and took advantage of the wars in Greece. Within 50 years of the end of the Peloponnesian War, the Macedonians had conquered many of the Greek states (see page 72).

Key dates

479-431BC The Golden Age of Athens.

460BC The Spartans reject Athenian help in stopping a rebellion. The Athenians start to build the Long Walls.

431BC Start of the Peloponnesian War.

415-413BC Athens sends an expedition to Sicily which is defeated.

405BC The Spartans defeat the Athenian fleet at the Battle of Aegospotami.

404BC The Athenians surrender. End of the Peloponnesian War.

371BC The Spartans are defeated by the Thebans at the Battle of Leuctra and Thebes becomes a leading power in Greece.

362BC The Thebans are defeated by the Spartans and Athenians at the Battle of Mantinea.

Gods and goddesses

The Greeks believed in many divine beings who looked after all aspects of life and death. They thought of the gods as being rather like humans.

They believed the gods got married, had children, and showed human emotions like love or anger. The gods' personalities featured in many legends.

How the world began

According to legend, Gaea (Mother Earth) rose out of chaos. She gave birth to a son, Uranos (Sky), who became her husband. They had many children, the most important of whom were the fourteen Titans. One of them, Cronos, led the others in a rebellion against their father and deposed him.

Cronos married his sister, Rhea. Their youngest son, Zeus, led his brothers and sisters against the Titans. He deposed Cronos and became the leader of the new gods, The new rulers lived on Mount Olympus and were known as the Olympians.

The battle between the Titans and the Olympians

The Olympian gods

This family tree shows some of the Greek deities. The most important gods were the 12 Olympians, whose names are written in capitals. Some of the legends associated with them are told below. Most of the gods had their own special symbols.

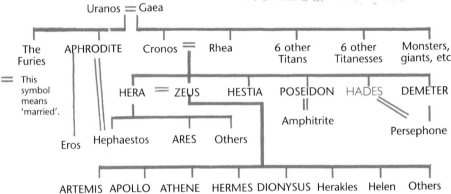

Zeus

Zeus was the ruler of the gods and controlled the heavens. He was married to his sister Hera, and was often unfaithful to her. He had many affairs with mortal women and appeared to them in various disguises, such as a bull, a shower of gold or a swan.

Zeus' symbols: the thunderbolt, eagle and oak tree

Hera

Hera was the sister and wife of Zeus. She was the protector of women and of marriage. She was beautiful and proud, and bitterly resented her husband's affairs with other women. She often persecuted his lovers and their children.

Hera's symbols: the pomegranate and the peacock

Poseidon

Poseidon was the brother of Zeus and ruler of the seas. He lived in an underwater palace, where he kept his gold chariot and white horses. Poseidon was also known as the earth-shaker, because he was thought to cause earthquakes.

Poseidon's symbols: the trident, dolphins and horses

Hestia

Hestia was the goddess of the hearth. Every Greek city and family had a shrine dedicated to her. She was gentle and pure, and stood aloof from the constant quarrels of the other gods. Eventually she resigned her throne on Olympus, knowing she would receive a welcome wherever she went.

Hades

Hades ruled the Underworld, the Kingdom of the Dead. He guarded the dead jealously, rarely letting anyone return to Earth. He owned all the precious metals and gems on Earth. Hades kidnapped and married his niece Persephone.

Hades drove a gold chariot with black horses.

Demeter's symbol: a sheaf of wheat or barley

Demeter

Demeter was the goddess of all plants. When her daughter Persephone was kidnapped, Demeter went to search for her. This caused winter. You can read the full story of Persephone on page 82.

Aphrodite

Aphrodite was the goddess of love and beauty. Born in the sea, she rode to shore on a seashell. Aphrodite was married to Hephaestos, but loved Ares. She wore a golden belt which made her irresistibly attractive.

Aphrodite's symbols: roses, doves, sparrows, dolphins and rams

Hephaestos

Hephaestos was a smith who built Zeus a golden throne and a shield, which caused storms and thunder when it was shaken. He was the patron deity of craftsmen and the long-suffering husband of Aphrodite.

Ares

Ares was the god of war and Aphrodite's lover. He was short-tempered and violent. He once had to stand trial for murder in Athens on the hill of the Areopagus, which was named after him by the Greeks.

Ares' symbols: a burning torch, spear, dogs and vultures

Artemis' symbols: cypress trees, deer and dogs

Artemis

Artemis was the moon goddess. Her silver arrows brought plague and death, though she could heal as well. She protected young girls and pregnant women. Artemis was the mistress of all wild animals and enjoyed hunting in her chariot pulled by stags.

Apollo

Apollo was the twin brother of Artemis. He was the god of the sun, light and truth, and he also controlled music, poetry, science and healing. Apollo killed his mother's enemy the serpent Python when it was sheltering in the shrine at Delphi. He seized the shrine and made Delphi his Oracle (see page 68).

Apollo's symbol: the laurel tree

Hermes

Hermes was a naughty child, full of tricks and cunning. He stole cattle from Apollo, but invented the lyre to appease him. He became the messenger of the gods. He was said to have invented the alphabet, mathematics, astronomy and boxing.

Hermes wore a winged hat and sandals, and carried a staff.

Athene

Daughter of Zeus and Metis the Titaness, Athene was goddess of wisdom and war, and patron deity of Athens. Zeus swallowed Metis because of a prophecy that if she had a son he would depose his father. One day Zeus had a headache so he ordered that his skull be split open. Athene sprang out.

Athene's symbols: the owl and the olive tree

Dionysus

Dionysus was god of the vine, wine and fertility. He wandered the world teaching people how to make wine. When Hestia resigned her place on Olympus, Dionysus became one of the 12 Olympians.

Dionysus carried a special staff, known as a *thyrsus*.

For a link to a website where you can see computer animations of the Acropolis in Athens, and watch a short movie about the Parthenon, go to **www.usborne-quicklinks.com**

Temples, worship and festivals

The Greeks believed that gods needed somewhere to live on Earth, so they built temples for them.

The basic design of temples developed from the royal halls of the Mycenaean Age.

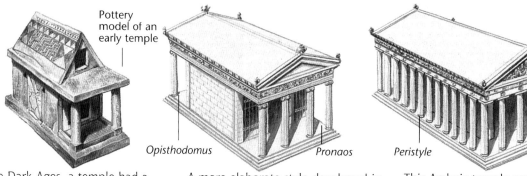

Pottery model of an early temple

Opisthodomus   *Pronaos*   *Peristyle*

In the Dark Ages, a temple had a room, called a *cella*, with a porch in front. The *cella* contained a statue of the god, known as the cult statue.

A more elaborate style developed in the Archaic Period. The front porch was known as the *pronaos*, and the back porch as the *opisthodomus*.

This Archaic temple was built on a platform, and had steps up to the entrance. Around the outside was a row of columns, called a *peristyle*.

The Parthenon

In the Classical Period temples became much larger and more elaborate. This reconstruction shows the Parthenon in Athens, which was built in 447-438BC.

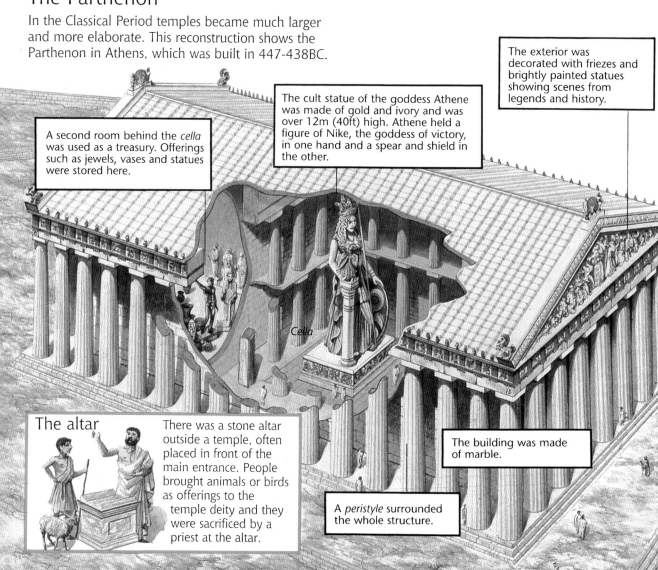

The exterior was decorated with friezes and brightly painted statues showing scenes from legends and history.

The cult statue of the goddess Athene was made of gold and ivory and was over 12m (40ft) high. Athene held a figure of Nike, the goddess of victory, in one hand and a spear and shield in the other.

A second room behind the *cella* was used as a treasury. Offerings such as jewels, vases and statues were stored here.

Cella

The altar

There was a stone altar outside a temple, often placed in front of the main entrance. People brought animals or birds as offerings to the temple deity and they were sacrificed by a priest at the altar.

The building was made of marble.

A *peristyle* surrounded the whole structure.

Festivals

The Greeks held many festivals in praise of their gods. The purpose of a festival was to please the gods and persuade them to grant people's wishes. This could be by making crops grow or bringing victory in war. Festivals did not only consist of religious ceremonies – events such as athletic competitions or theatrical performances could also be held. These events included things which would please the particular god. For example, at the Pythian Games, dedicated to Apollo, winners received crowns made of laurel, which was Apollo's sacred plant.

Important citizens

Musicians and dancers

Offerings

Soldiers

A dress for the statue of the goddess Athene was displayed on the mast of a ship, which was dragged along in the procession.

Priests and priestesses

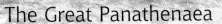

The festival was a public holiday, so that everyone could watch the procession.

Sacrificial beasts

The Great Panathenaea

The most important festival in Athens was the *Great Panathenaea*, the feast of the goddess Athene. It was held every four years and lasted for six days. It included music, poetry recitals and sports events. The climax of the festival was a procession from the Dipylon Gate to the Acropolis. There a specially made dress was offered to a statue of Athene, which was said to have fallen from heaven in ancient times.

The Anthesteria

A festival called the *Anthesteria* was held in Athens each February. Wine from the last harvest was put on sale and a statue of Dionysus, god of wine, was carried to his temple. On the final day of the festival, each family cooked a meal for the spirits of the dead and left it on the altar in their house.

During the *Anthesteria*, children were given special jugs.

Worship

Private worship played an important part in Greek religion. A family would say prayers every day at the altar in their house. During prayers an offering of wine, known as a *libation*, was poured over the altar.

People would also pray to the appropriate gods as they went about their daily life.

If someone wanted to ask the gods for something in particular, they would go to the temple of the appropriate deity and make a sacrifice. This could be cakes, a libation, a bird or an animal.

There were rules on how to please the various gods. For example, different species of birds and animals were preferred by different gods. If the rules were not followed, the offering might not be accepted. Each god had his or her own priests, who ensured sacrifices were made correctly.

Most gods were addressed with raised arms and hands turned up to heaven.

To worship Underworld gods, the palms faced the ground.

To address a sky god, the person had to face the east.

For a marine god, the person had to face the sea.

Oracles and mystery cults

The Greeks never began an important project without first trying to learn the will of the gods. Often they would visit an oracle, where a special priest or priestess could speak on behalf of a god.

Other popular ways of learning what the future might hold were reading omens or consulting a soothsayer (someone who could foresee the future).

Oracles

The word oracle can mean the priestess who spoke for the god, the sacred place where she was consulted, or the message she gave. There were several oracles in Greece. The most famous one was at Delphi, where Apollo was believed to speak through his priestess, the Pythia. At first, the Pythia gave oracles once a year, but Delphi became so popular that two priestesses gave oracles every week.

The temple priests put people's questions to the Pythia. Then they interpreted her replies, which were often very vague.

The Pythia gave her oracles in an inner sanctuary. First she bathed in a holy fountain, drank water from a sacred spring and inhaled the smoke of burning laurel leaves. This reconstruction shows how a consultation might have looked.

The inner sanctuary was closed off from the priests by a curtain.

The Pythia dressed in white and held a branch of laurel in her hand.

She gave her oracles in a trance, said to be caused by fumes rising from a natural cleft in the rocks.

Omens

Interpreting omens was a skilled art, and was only undertaken by trained priests. Omens could be read from different things, such as blemishes on the innards of sacrificed animals, the flight of birds or thunder and lightning.

Soothsayers

The Greeks believed that certain people, known as soothsayers, could foresee the future. According to legend, Cassandra, a princess of Troy who had these powers, broke a promise to Apollo. He decreed that no one would ever believe her again. Cassandra warned the people of Troy that the wooden horse was a trick, but they ignored her and the city was destroyed.

Fate

The Greeks believed that each person's destiny was decided by three goddesses called the Fates. Clotho spun the thread of life. Lachesis wound the thread and allotted a person's destiny, and Atropos cut the thread, causing a person to die.

Clotho   Lachesis   Atropos

Tyche, the goddess of fortune, could shower people with gifts from her horn of plenty. But she also juggled with a ball, showing how someone could be up one day, and down the next.

Mystery cults

Many Greeks who were looking for a deeper religious faith joined one of the mystery cults. These were secret groups associated with particular deities. The cults promised an answer to the meaning of life and a happy life after death.

People who undertook the necessary training were initiated (introduced) into the cult by stages. The most popular was the cult of the goddesses Demeter and Persephone at Eleusis. The cult's main initiation ceremony was called the Greater Mysteries.

The procession

The Greater Mysteries started with several days of sacrifices and purification. On the fifth day, a great procession set out from Athens to travel to Eleusis. They arrived at night, by torchlight.

Statue of the goddess

Priestesses carried the sacred objects of the cult in baskets on their heads.

The initiates wore white robes.

The initiation ceremony

No one knows exactly what happened at an initation ceremony because it took place in private and the initiates were sworn to secrecy. This reconstruction shows what may have happened during an initiation.

The priestess, holding a pomegranate, played Persephone.

People waiting to be initiated

There may have been an enactment of the deeds of the goddesses. This priestess played the part of Demeter.

People who had reached the higher stages of initiation, known as 'viewers', were probably shown something special, such as sacred cult objects.

The origin of the Eleusinian mysteries

The cult of Demeter and Persephone was founded by Prince Triptolemus of Eleusis. According to legend, when Persephone was kidnapped and taken to the Underworld, Demeter wandered the Earth searching for her, disguised as a poor old woman. When she arrived at Eleusis, the royal family took her in and gave her a job caring for the royal children. After Persephone was returned to Demeter, both goddesses returned to Eleusis.

They gave the king's son, Prince Triptolemus, a bag of grain and showed him how to plant and reap. Triptolemus went all over Greece teaching people how to grow grain. Then he built a temple at Eleusis and established the cult of Demeter and Persephone. You can read more of Persephone's story on page 82.

This carving shows Prince Triptolemus with the two goddesses.

For a link to a website where you can watch a short movie about ancient Greek funerals and the afterlife, go to **www.usborne-quicklinks.com**

Death and the Underworld

The Greeks believed that when people died, their souls went to the Underworld. This was an underground kingdom, sometimes known as Hades, after the god who ruled it. Many caves and fissures on Earth were thought to be entrances to the Underworld. The god Hermes guided souls through these entrances to a river known as the Styx, which marked the boundary between the world of the living and the Underworld. This picture gives some idea of what the Greeks thought would happen to them in the Underworld.

Souls were guided to the banks of the Styx by Hermes.

Souls whose relatives had provided them with a coin (see below) paid Charon the ferryman to take them across the river. Souls without the fare wandered comfortless on the bank.

Cerberus, the three-headed dog, stopped living intruders from entering the Underworld and preventing any of Hades' subjects from escaping.

Minos, Rhadamanthys and Aeacus judged all the newly-arrived souls, according to how the person had behaved in his or her earthly life.

Funerals

Greek funerals were designed to ensure that the soul arrived safely in the Underworld. Many Greeks believed that, without the proper rituals, the soul would wander on the banks of the Styx and would not be able to enter the Underworld.

Even after the funeral, the continued well-being of the dead depended to some extent on the care of the living. Families made offerings to their ancestors on the anniversaries of their births and deaths, and at special festivals for the dead.

Visitors washed when they left, as death was thought to be unclean.

Wealthy families hired musicians and professional mourners to join the procession.

When someone died, their relatives and friends wore black and women cut their hair short as signs of mourning. The dead body lay in state at home for a day, so that people could come to pay their respects. The body was carefully dressed and arranged. A coin was placed in its mouth to enable the soul to pay the fare to cross the Styx.

Early on the morning of the funeral a procession formed at the dead person's house. The body was either placed on a cart or on a bier carried by the relatives and friends. The body was then taken to the cemetery. The procession was a noisy affair, as it was the custom to express grief publicly with tears, sobbing and wailing.

Souls of initiates could ask to be born again. If they got to the Elysian Fields three times, they could then go to the Isles of the Blessed, a place of eternal joy.

The Pool of Memory

People who had led virtuous lives, along with initiates of the mystery cults, went to the Elysian Fields, a happy place filled with sunlight.

The souls of people who had led wicked lives were condemned to eternal punishment in Tartarus.

Another road led to Erebus, the palace of Hades and Persephone. By the palace were two pools.

The Palace of Pluto and Persephone

The Pool of Memory enabled initiates from the mystery cults to remember the secrets of the cult and pass straight to the Elysian Fields.

Most people had not been very good or very bad and were sent to the Asphodel Fields. This was a grey, boring place where the souls waited for offerings from the living to cheer them up.

Ordinary souls drank at the Pool of Lethe (forgetfulness).

Tombs

Cemeteries were usually situated outside the city walls. Each family had its own burial plot, where members of the family were either buried or cremated. Early tombs were marked with a plain marble slab, topped with a sculptured decoration. A rich person would be buried in a stone coffin known as a *sarcophagus*.

Plain marble slabs like these were set up to mark early tombs.

It was the custom to bury personal belongings, such as jewels and clothes, with the dead person. Food, drink and bronze or pottery vessels were also buried for the soul to use in the afterlife. By the 5th century BC, people who could afford it built elaborate tombs which looked like small temples. These were often decorated with portraits of the dead person carved on stone slabs, known *stelae*.

Stele

Lekythoi

A *sarcophagus* often had elaborately carved reliefs on the sides.

The women of the family continued to bring offerings to the tomb after the funeral. Perfume was often offered to the dead. It was carried in vases known as *lekythoi*.

The rise of Macedonia

Macedonia lies in the northeast of Greece (see map below). The Macedonians claimed to be descendants of Macedon, son of Zeus. Although they thought of themselves as Greek, many Greeks considered the Macedonians to be little better than barbarians. Although the Macedonians spoke Greek, they had such a strong accent that it was said to be impossible to understand them.

During the 6th and 5th centuries BC, Macedonia was invaded many times. In 399BC the king was murdered and the country entered 40 years of instability and civil war.

This ended with the accession of Philip II in 359BC. When he came to the throne, Macedonia had lost a lot of its territory and was split by political rivalries. Many of its soldiers had been killed and the country was impoverished.

Small ivory head of Philip, found in his tomb

Within 25 years Philip had united the country and turned Macedonia into the greatest military power of the day. He was a brilliant soldier, a fine speaker and a cunning diplomat with great charm. Even so, critics, such as the Athenian politician Demosthenes, saw him as a threat to democracy and independence.

A gold medallion showing Philip's wife Olympias

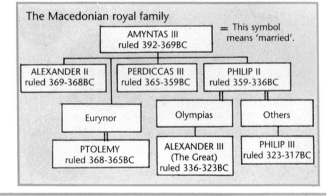

The Macedonian royal family

	AMYNTAS III ruled 392-369BC	= This symbol means 'married'.

ALEXANDER II ruled 369-368BC	PERDICCAS III ruled 365-359BC	PHILIP II ruled 359-336BC

Eurynor	Olympias	Others

PTOLEMY ruled 368-365BC	ALEXANDER III (The Great) ruled 336-323BC	PHILIP III ruled 323-317BC

Philip's conquests

Philip quickly brought Macedonia under control. In 357BC he started to expand his territory and by 342BC he controlled all of Thrace, Chalkidike and Thessaly (see map). In 342BC, the remaining Greek states, led by Athens and Thebes, formed the Hellenic League against him.

Philip defeated them in 338BC at the Battle of Chaeronea and gained control of Greece. He joined all the Greek states together in the League of Corinth, of which he was the *hegemon*, or leader. In 337BC he united Greece and Macedonia in a common cause by announcing a war against Persia.

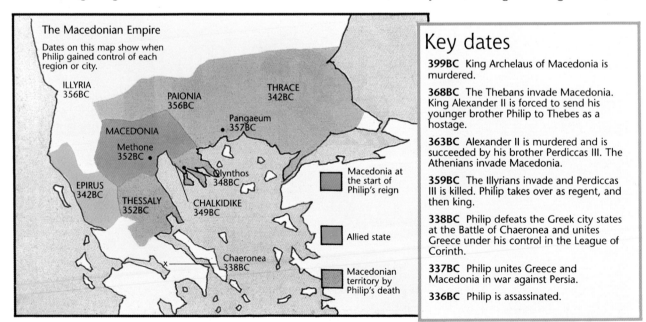

The Macedonian Empire

Dates on this map show when Philip gained control of each region or city.

ILLYRIA 356BC
PAIONIA 356BC
THRACE 342BC
Pangaeum 357BC
MACEDONIA
Methone 352BC
Olynthos 348BC
EPIRUS 342BC
THESSALY 352BC
CHALKIDIKE 349BC
Chaeronea 338BC

Macedonia at the start of Philip's reign

Allied state

Macedonian territory by Philip's death

Key dates

399BC King Archelaus of Macedonia is murdered.

368BC The Thebans invade Macedonia. King Alexander II is forced to send his younger brother Philip to Thebes as a hostage.

363BC Alexander II is murdered and is succeeded by his brother Perdiccas III. The Athenians invade Macedonia.

359BC The Illyrians invade and Perdiccas III is killed. Philip takes over as regent, and then king.

338BC Philip defeats the Greek city states at the Battle of Chaeronea and unites Greece under his control in the League of Corinth.

337BC Philip unites Greece and Macedonia in war against Persia.

336BC Philip is assassinated.

For a link to a website where you can view an exhibit of objects found in Philip's tomb, go to **www.usborne-quicklinks.com**

The army

At the beginning of his reign, Philip reorganized the army and began an intensive training schedule.

This produced a tough, well-disciplined army which was the most effective fighting force of the day.

Soldiers at the back held their spears upright.

Soldiers in the first ranks held their spears out in front of them.

Each soldier was armed with a short sword and a long spear known as a *sarissa*.

The Macedonian infantry originally consisted of lightly-armed *peltasts* (see page 37). Philip gave them heavier body protection and long spears, and taught them to fight in a phalanx, shown above. They attacked by charging into the enemy's lines with their spears extended. This was a very effective tactic and proved to be a decisive factor in Philip's military successes.

There were elite units called the Companion Infantry and the Companion Cavalry. The sons of Macedonian noblemen were often educated at court and served as royal pages before joining the Companion Cavalry. The mosaic above shows two royal pages out hunting. Philip made great use of the Companion Cavalry, which he developed from the king's mounted bodyguard.

The Companion Cavalry wore cuirasses and helmets, and were armed with long spears and swords.

Philip's death

Philip had several wives, but only one queen, Olympias. Her son Alexander was accepted as Philip's heir. In 337BC, Philip took another wife, Cleopatra, and set Olympias aside. He was assassinated soon after. The assassin could have been a political opponent, but it was also possible that Olympias or Alexander were responsible.

In AD1977 archaeologists discovered a new tomb in the royal graveyard at Vergina. In the inner chamber they found a casket, containing the cremated remains of a man aged 40-50.

Experts have since been able to piece together the skull. It had a hole near the right eye. This almost certainly proves that it was Philip, who had been hit in the face by an arrow and lost his right eye.

This cutaway reconstruction shows Philip's tomb and some of the treasures that were found in it.

This gold casket held Philip's ashes. The star symbol was the emblem of the Macedonian royal family.

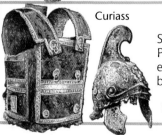

Curiass

Several pieces of Philip's military equipment were buried with him.

Helmet

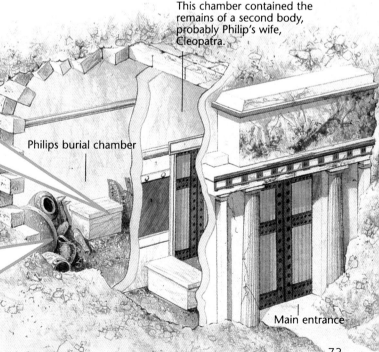

This chamber contained the remains of a second body, probably Philip's wife, Cleopatra.

Philips burial chamber

Main entrance

Alexander the Great

Alexander became King of Macedonia in 336BC after the murder of his father, Philip. He was only 20. He immediately embarked on a career of military conquests, which gained him the largest empire the ancient world had known, and earned him the title of Alexander the Great. He was a military genius, who inspired great loyalty in his followers and who had extraordinary courage.

In 334BC, Alexander led 35,000 troops into Asia Minor to attack the Persians. This began an 11-year campaign, during which he captured vast territories in Asia Minor, Egypt, Afghanistan, Iran and India.

This reconstruction shows the Battle of Issus (333BC), where Alexander defeated the Persians. It is based on a Roman mosaic in Pompeii.

Picture of Alexander taken from a Roman mosaic

Alexander founded many new cities, most of which he named 'Alexandria', after himself. The most famous of these was the port of Alexandria in Egypt, which became the country's new capital.

Alexander did little to change the administration of the lands he seized, although he usually replaced the local governors with his own men. He left Greeks behind in all the areas he conquered, which helped to spread Greek language and culture across an enormous area. This Greek influence lasted long after Alexander's empire had collapsed.

Alexander realized that his empire was too big to be administered from Greece. In Persia, he tried to include Persians in the government to help unify the empire. He planned to give them equal rights and to let them serve in the army. The whole empire was to have one currency, and use Greek as the official language. Alexander himself adopted Persian dress and married a Persian noblewoman named Roxane.

In 323BC, Alexander died suddenly of a fever. He does not seem to have made plans for the government of the empire after his death. Roxane was pregnant with Alexander's heir, but his generals divided the empire up between themselves.

Alexander was often shown on coins of the time.

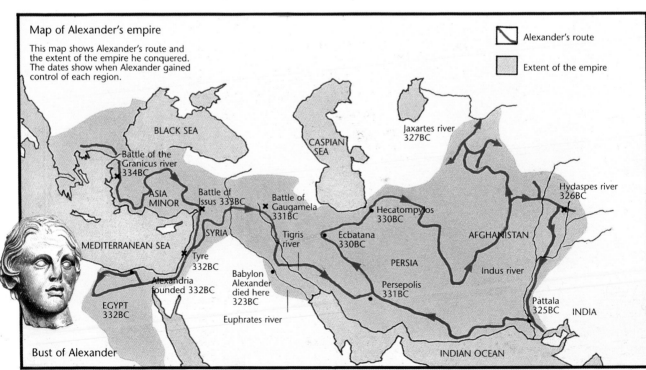

Map of Alexander's empire

This map shows Alexander's route and the extent of the empire he conquered. The dates show when Alexander gained control of each region.

Alexander's route

Extent of the empire

BLACK SEA

CASPIAN SEA

Jaxartes river 327BC

Battle of the Granicus river 334BC

ASIA MINOR

Battle of Issus 333BC

Battle of Gaugamela 331BC

Hecatompylos 330BC

Hydaspes river 326BC

AFGHANISTAN

SYRIA

Tigris river

Ecbatana 330BC

MEDITERRANEAN SEA

Tyre 332BC

Alexandria founded 332BC

Babylon Alexander died here 323BC

PERSIA

Indus river

Persepolis 331BC

Pattala 325BC

INDIA

EGYPT 332BC

Euphrates river

Bust of Alexander

INDIAN OCEAN

Alexander's army

Alexander inherited a large, well-trained army with high morale. He invaded Persia with an army of 30,000 infantry and 5000 cavalry.

Macedonian troops formed the core of the army. It also contained troops from conquered provinces, and professional soldiers from all over Greece.

The cavalry

The basic cavalry unit consisted of 49 men. It charged in a wedge-shaped formation with the commander in front. The cavalry was usually used to break up a phalanx of enemy foot soldiers.

The cavalry often attacked by charging at the right end of the phalanx, which was its weakest point (see page 37). A phalanx of foot soldiers could then move in from behind in hand-to-hand fighting.

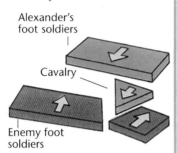

Alexander's foot soldiers

Cavalry

Enemy foot soldiers

The cavalry was mostly made up of horsemen from Thessaly, with troops from the states of the Corinthian League. The elite troops, or Companion Cavalry, consisted of eight squadrons of Macedonian noblemen.

Cavalryman from Thessaly

Member of the Companion Cavalry

The infantry

The infantry was made up of foot soldiers, javelin throwers, archers and slingers. Alexander continued to use the Companion Infantry, and he also had a bodyguard known as the *hypaspists*.

Foot soldiers continued to fight in a phalanx. Alexander often used the phalanx in an oblique formation, shown here. It enabled him to attack the weaker right wing of an enemy phalanx.

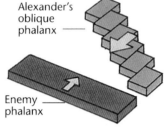

Alexander's oblique phalanx

Enemy phalanx

Under Alexander, many infantry soldiers went back to using the heavy bronze curiass and shield of the Greek *hoplites*, although they still carried the Macedonian *sarissa* (spear). This picture shows a member of the Companion Infantry.

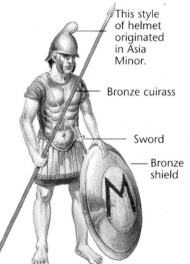

This style of helmet originated in Asia Minor.

Bronze cuirass

Sword

Bronze shield

Sarissa

The army on the move

Each soldier was expected to carry all his own weapons, as well as a personal pack containing bedding and cooking equipment. Pack animals and baggage wagons were used to carry bulky equipment such as tents, water skins and siege equipment, and to move wounded men. The army was accompanied by servants and grooms, and by many women and children.

Key dates

336BC Philip is murdered and Alexander comes to the Macedonian throne.

334BC Alexander invades Persia. He defeats the Persian governors of Asia Minor at the Battle of the Granicus river.

333BC Alexander defeats the Persians, led by King Darius, at the Battle of Issus.

332BC Siege and destruction of the city of Tyre in the Lebanon. Alexander conquers Egypt and founds the city of Alexandria.

331BC Alexander defeats the Persians at the Battle of Gaugamela and becomes King of Persia.

327BC Alexander invades India.

326BC Alexander defeats the Indian King Porus at the Battle of the Hydaspes river.

323BC Alexander dies in Babylon.

The Hellenistic World

For several hundred years after Alexander's death, Greek culture and ideas dominated the countries of his empire. The period from 336-30BC is known as the Hellenistic Age, from the Greek word *Hellene*, which means 'Greek'.

When news of Alexander's death reached Greece, many cities rebelled against the Macedonians. This began the Lamian War (323-322BC).

The Greeks had some victories, but were beaten by Macedonian troops returning from Asia.

Alexander was succeeded by his infant son and his half-brother Philip Arrideus. Alexander's generals, known as the *Diadochi*, or 'successors', ruled on behalf of the two kings. But the *Diadochi* soon divided the empire up between themselves and this led to wars that lasted from 323-281BC.

Alexander became a legend. This Persian picture shows him in a flying machine.

The division of the empire

By 301BC, Alexander's mother, wife, son and half-brother had all been murdered in the struggle for power. After the Battle of Ipsus in 301BC, four kingdoms were established, with the rival *Diadochi* as kings. Finally, in 281BC, three kingdoms emerged (see map). They were ruled by the descendants of three of the *Diadochi*: Ptolemy, Antigonas and Seleucus.

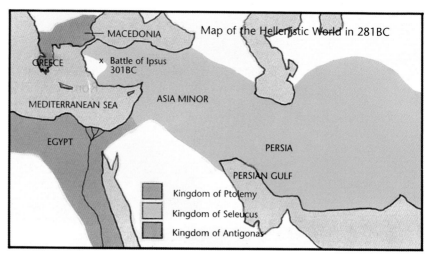

Map of the Hellenistic World in 281BC

MACEDONIA
GREECE
x Battle of Ipsus 301BC
MEDITERRANEAN SEA
ASIA MINOR
EGYPT
PERSIA
PERSIAN GULF

Kingdom of Ptolemy
Kingdom of Seleucus
Kingdom of Antigonas

Macedonia and Greece: 281-146BC

The Antigonids became the new Macedonian royal family. They ruled Greece from Macedonia, and ran the country by keeping soldiers in the major cities. In 229BC Athens bribed its garrison to leave and became a neutral state. It never regained its political importance, but Athens continued to be respected as the heart of Greek civilization.

During the third century BC, the Greek colonies in southern Italy became threatened by the Romans, who were expanding their territory throughout Italy (see opposite page). King Pyrrhus of Epirus went to the aid of the Greek colonists. He defeated the Romans twice, in 280BC and 279BC, but withdrew after a third battle in 275BC.

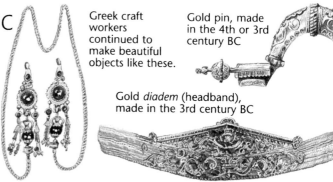

Greek craft workers continued to make beautiful objects like these.

Gold pin, made in the 4th or 3rd century BC

Gold *diadem* (headband), made in the 3rd century BC

Gold earrings from the 1st century BC

When the Romans occupied Greece they stole many works of art and took them back to Italy.

Conflict with the Romans continued when King Philip V of Macedonia helped the Carthaginian general Hannibal in his fight against Rome. This provoked Roman reprisals, which led to three Macedonian Wars between the Antigonids and the Romans (215-205BC, 200-197BC and 179-168BC).

In 168BC the Macedonians were defeated at the Battle of Pydna. After a Macedonian revolt in 147-146BC, the Romans put Macedonia and Greece under direct rule as provinces of the Roman empire.

The Seleucids: 304-64BC

The Seleucids seized an enormous area of Alexander's empire, but it proved impossible to hold together. Despite inviting Greek settlers, the Seleucids never had enough manpower to control all their provinces, and by 180BC the Seleucids' territory had been greatly reduced (see map).

Wars with the Parthians, rebellions and disputed successions to the throne caused the gradual decay of the rest of the empire.

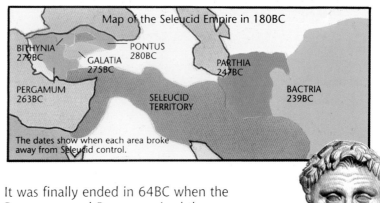

Map of the Seleucid Empire in 180BC

BITHYNIA 279BC
GALATIA 275BC
PONTUS 280BC
PARTHIA 247BC
PERGAMUM 263BC
SELEUCID TERRITORY
BACTRIA 239BC

The dates show when each area broke away from Seleucid control.

It was finally ended in 64BC when the Roman general Pompey seized the Seleucid lands and they were incorporated into the Roman empire.

Roman bust of Pompey

The Ptolemaic empire: 323-30BC

Ptolemy was in many ways the most successful of the *Diadochi*. He had contented himself with taking just Egypt, and as a result kept his kingdom intact. At the start of his reign, he gained great prestige by having Alexander's body buried in Alexandria, which became the capital city of his empire. Ptolemy and his successors governed Egypt from 323-30BC. They always preserved their Greek culture, and only the last ruler of the dynasty, Cleopatra VII, learned the Egyptian language.

Egyptian carving of Ptolemy

Confusion over the succession and increasing Roman involvement in Egyptian affairs destroyed the Ptolemy dynasty. Queen Cleopatra VII and her Roman lover Mark Antony were defeated by the Romans in 31BC. Egypt, the last Hellenistic Kingdom, became a Roman province in 30BC.

The Ptolemies introduced many Greek things to Egypt. This mosaic shows an Egyptian warship, which was based on a Greek trireme.

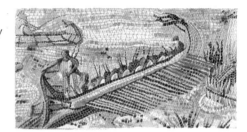

The Romans

The Romans developed from a tribe from central Europe who settled around the Tiber river in Italy in c.1000BC. By around 250BC they controlled most of Italy. They began to expand their territory abroad and, thanks to their military efficiency, soon built a large empire (see map).

The Romans eventually conquered all the Hellenistic kingdoms and were greatly influenced by the Greek ideas they met there. They adopted many aspects of Greek life, such as architecture, literature, religion and social customs. This helped keep Greek culture alive.

The arch of Constantine in Rome

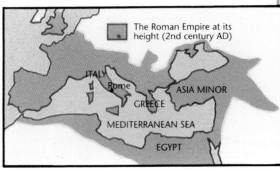

The Roman Empire at its height (2nd century AD)

ITALY
Rome
GREECE
ASIA MINOR
MEDITERRANEAN SEA
EGYPT

Key dates

323-322BC The Greek states rebel against the Macedonians in the Lamian War, but are defeated.

323-281BC Wars of the *Diadochi*, ending in the establishment of three *Diadochi* kingdoms.

275BC Greek colonies in southern Italy pass to the Romans after the defeat of King Pyrrhus of Epirus.

168BC King Perseus of Macedonia is defeated by the Romans at the Battle of Pydna. The Macedonian monarchy is abolished.

147-146BC The Romans suppress a Macedonian revolt. Macedonia and Greece become provinces of the Roman empire.

64BC The Seleucid empire is conquered by the Roman general Pompey and becomes a Roman province.

31-30BC Cleopatra VII of Egypt is defeated by the Romans at the Battle of Actium and Egypt becomes a Roman province.

For a link to a website where you can read more about the life and work of Socrates, go to **www.usborne-quicklinks.com**

Learning

Early Greeks used stories about the gods to answer questions on how the world worked or the purpose of life. In the 6th century BC some people began to look for more practical explanations. They did this by making observations about the world around them.

The Greeks named these scholars *philosophers*, or 'lovers of knowledge'. Today we think of philosophy as the study of the nature of the universe and human life. But early Greek philosophers also studied subjects such as biology, mathematics and astronomy.

Scientists and inventors

By observing how things worked, philosophers were able to make many new scientific discoveries.

Some of these discoveries have provided the foundations of modern science.

The astronomer Aristarchus deduced that the Earth revolved on its axis and that it moved around the Sun. His idea wasn't accepted as he could not produce evidence to prove it.

Archimedes discovered an important law of physics. One day he got into a bath and the water overflowed. From this he deduced that an object displaces its own volume of water.

Thales of Miletus calculated the height of one of the Egyptian pyramids by measuring its shadow. He is also said to have been able to predict an eclipse of the Sun.

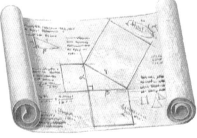

Anaximander deduced that much of the land had once been covered in water. He also believed that humans had not appeared on Earth in their present form, but had developed from an earlier creature, perhaps a fish. Another scholar, Xenophanes, discovered that fossils were the remains of plants and animals preserved in rock.

Greek scholars, such as Pythagoras, Euclid and Archimedes, worked out many basic rules of mathematics. They devised theorems which are still used in geometry. These include Pythagoras' theorem on triangles and the use of pi in working out the circumference or area of a circle.

Another astronomer, Anaxagoras, realized that the Moon didn't produce light itself, but reflected the light of the Sun. He also discovered that eclipses were caused by the Moon passing between the Earth and the Sun and blocking the light.

The Museum

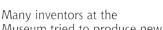

Crossbow

In the Hellenistic Period a temple to the Muses (see page 54) was built at Alexandria in Egypt. It was known as the Museum. Scholars from all over the Greek world worked there. The Museum also had a library which contained every important Greek book, as well as translations of many foreign books.

We know that engineers at the Museum invented some interesting devices, many of which used water or steam power. However, some of these machines were not very practical and were never widely used. Two of the more useful ones are shown on the right.

Many inventors at the Museum tried to produce new weapons. These were mostly catapults and crossbows.

Archimedes' screw

Archimedes built a device which raised water from one level to another. It was in the form of a large screw. Water rose through the screw as it was turned. Pumps like this are still used in parts of Africa today.

Political and moral philosophers

Philosphers also thought about how people should behave or what the ideal political systems would be. Their ideas form the basis of modern philosophy. Here are some of the most important thinkers.

Pythagoras, a mathematician from Samos, founded a sacred community in Italy. He was interested in what happened to people after they died. He taught that, at death, the soul passed into another creature and so was born again.

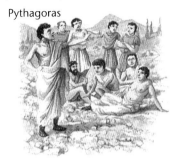
Pythagoras

Socrates thought that people would behave well if they knew what good conduct was. He challenged people to think about good and evil, which made him unpopular with some Athenians. They charged him with disobeying religious laws and he was forced to kill himself.

Socrates

Socrates never wrote down his ideas. They were reported by his pupils, one of whom was Plato. In his own work, Plato tried to find the ideal way of governing a state.

Plato

Aristotle was born in 384BC and was a pupil of Plato. He too was interested in man and society, and finding the ideal way to run a city-state. One of his pupils was Alexander the Great.

Aristotle

In the 4th century BC, Diogenes founded the school of philosophers known as Cynics. He had no respect for the rules of society and lived very simply. At one point his home was a large storage jar. He attacked dishonesty and excessive wealth.

Diogenes

The Stoic philosophers were named after the *stoa* (porch) where their founder Xenon taught. He believed that if people acted naturally they would behave well, as their nature was determined by the gods.

Xenon

Historians

The earliest Greeks had little interest in the past of other peoples. But in the 6th century BC, when they were threatened by the Persians, the Greeks realized they needed to know more about their opponents. Writers began to gather facts about the Persians, and others, but they weren't always accurate. It wasn't until the 5th century BC that reliable material on the Greeks and other peoples was recorded.

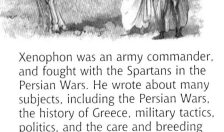

Herodotus is considered to be the first true historian and is often known as the 'Father of History'. He wrote a history of the Persian Wars after interviewing survivors and their families. He also went to other lands and wrote about peoples such as the Persians and Egyptians.

Another important historian was Thucydides. He wrote a history of the Peloponnesian War, which is regarded as one of the finest early works of history. Thucydides fought in the war himself and he also interviewed other people who had taken part.

Xenophon was an army commander, and fought with the Spartans in the Persian Wars. He wrote about many subjects, including the Persian Wars, the history of Greece, military tactics, politics, and the care and breeding of horses.

Medicine

Many Greek doctors were priests of Asclepius, the god of healing. By 420BC the cult of Asclepius had been established in Athens, where a festival known as the *Epidauria* was dedicated to him. Soon there were temples to him all over the Greek world.

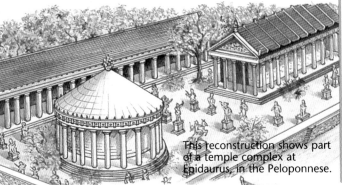

This reconstruction shows part of a temple complex at Epidaurus, in the Peloponnese.

Asclepius

According to legend, Asclepius was the son of Apollo. He was brought up by a *centaur* (a creature that was half man, half horse), who taught him medicine. The goddess Athene gave Asclepius two bottles of magic blood. The blood in one bottle would kill anything, but that in the other would bring the dead back to life. Asclepius brought so many people back from the dead that Pluto, god of the Underworld, complained to Zeus. Zeus was angry with Asclepius and killed him. But he later relented, brought Asclepius back to life and made him a god.

A statue of Asclepius with a snake, the symbol of medicine

Religious cures

People who were cured left an offering to Asclepius. This was often a model of the part of the body that had been cured. This relief shows a man making an offering of a model leg.

When people were ill, they went to a temple of Asclepius. There priests offered medicines, but also the hope of a miraculous cure. Sick people performed purification ceremonies.

Then they slept for a night in the god's temple, in the hope that Asclepius would heal them as they slept. Sometimes he might appear in a dream to reveal a cure.

Developments in medicine

Later, some doctors adopted a more scientific approach to medicine. They tried to use practical cures rather than religious ones, though they still respected Asclepius.

The founder of this movement was Hippocrates of Kos, who is thought to have lived around 460-377BC. His followers opened schools where this new type of medicine was taught.

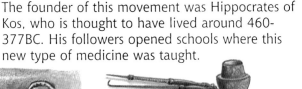

Surgical instruments from the Hellenistic Period

The new doctors did not believe that illness was a punishment from the gods. They searched for the causes of disease and tried to find out how the body worked. This relief shows a doctor examining a patient.

Doctors prescribed herbal medicines, a special diet, rest or gentle exercise. Sometimes they removed some blood, as it was thought to contain the disease. This vase shows a doctor taking blood from a patient's arm.

As there were no anaesthetics, operations were extremely painful and dangerous. Even if they survived, patients often died of infected wounds. Doctors tried to avoid operations whenever possible.

Map of ancient Greece

This map shows ancient Greece and the surrounding area. All the cities and regions mentioned in the book are marked on this map.

The names of regions or countries are written in capital letters. Cities are written in small letters and their positions are marked by dots.

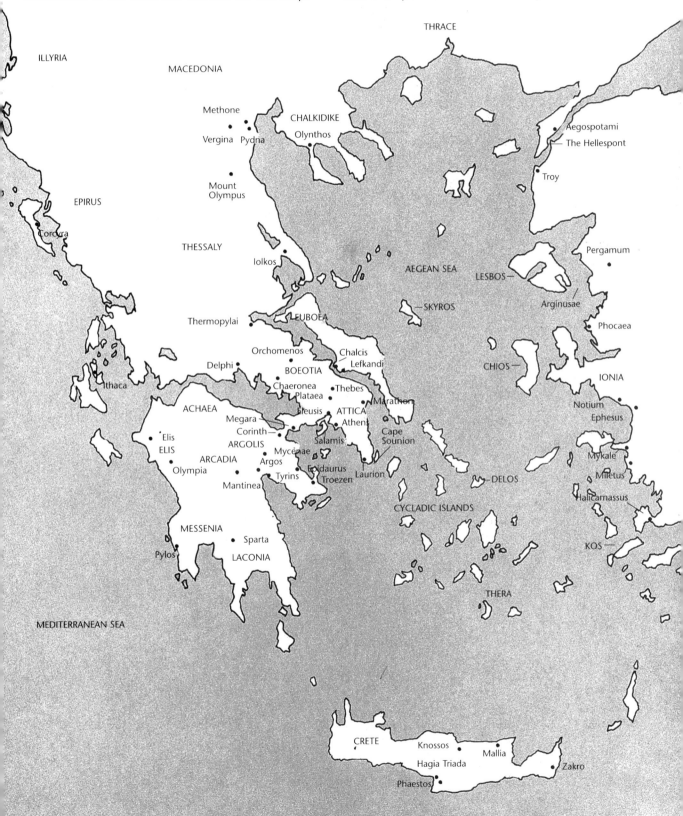

THRACE

ILLYRIA

MACEDONIA

Methone

CHALKIDIKE

Olynthos

Aegospotami

The Hellespont

Vergina Pydna

Troy

Mount Olympus

EPIRUS

Pergamum

Corcyra

THESSALY

Iolkos

AEGEAN SEA

LESBOS

Arginusae

SKYROS

Thermopylai

EUBOEA

Phocaea

Orchomenos

Chalcis

Lefkandi

CHIOS

Delphi

BOEOTIA

IONIA

Chaeronea

Plataea

Thebes

Ithaca

Eleusis

Marathon

ACHAEA

Megara

ATTICA

Notium

Ephesus

Corinth

Athens

Cape Sounion

Elis

ARGOLIS

Salamis

Mycenae

ELIS

ARCADIA

Argos

DELOS

Mykale

Miletus

Olympia

Epidaurus

Tyrins

Troezen

Laurion

Halicarnassus

Mantinea

CYCLADIC ISLANDS

MESSENIA

Sparta

KOS

Pylos

LACONIA

THERA

MEDITERRANEAN SEA

CRETE

Knossos

Mallia

Hagia Triada

Zakro

Phaestos

Greek myths and legends

The earliest Greeks had many myths – stories about gods and goddesses – which they told to explain the world around them. Later, many legends developed which described the lives and deeds of famous heroes in Greek history.

Below are some of the most important Greek myths and legends. Important names appear in **bold type** to make the main characters easier to identify. You can also read more about the most important gods and goddesses on pages 64-65.

Demeter and Persephone

Demeter, the goddess of crops and harvests, had a beautiful daughter named **Persephone**, **Hades**, the god of the Underworld, caught sight of Persephone one day and fell in love with her. He had been unable to find a wife, as nobody wanted to live with him in the Underworld where the sun never shone. So he decided to kidnap Persephone and make her his queen. He drove by in his chariot, seized her and carried her off.

Zeus intervenes

Demeter was very upset when she realized her daughter had disappeared. She neglected the plants and trees to look of Persephone. When she found out what had happened, she pleaded with **Zeus** to make Hades release her daughter. Zeus promised to help her, because no crops would grow and people were starving. So he decreed that Hades should let Persephone go, on condition that she had not tasted the food of the dead while she had been in the Underworld.

Persephone returns

Persephone has been so miserable that she hadn't eaten anything, but just before he released her, Hades persuaded her to taste six pomegranate seeds. Zeus decided that she could return to Earth, but would have to spend six months of each year with Hades, one for each seed she had eaten. Persephone returned to her mother, who was delighted. The crops grew again and it was spring. After that, for half of every year, Persephone went backt o live with Hades. Demeter became so sad that all the crops died, and it was winter once more.

Theseus

Theseus was the son of **Aegeus**, the king of Athens. As a young man, Aegeus went to a place called Troezene and fell in love with a princess named **Aethra**. But he had to return to Athens and could not take Aethra with him, even though she was pregnant. Before he left, he buried his sword and sandals under a stone. Aegeus told Aethra that if she had a son, when he grew up he should lift the stone and take the sword and sandals to Athens, where he would be introduced to the people as Aegeus' son and heir. Aethra gave birth to a son, and named him **Theseus**.

Theseus travels to Athens

When he was old enough, Theseus found the sandals and sword and set off to Athens to find his father. When he arrived, he went to meet his father, but Aegeus' wife **Medea** saw him first. She knew he had come for his inheritance, and wanted to stop him. She handed Aegeus some wine to give to the stranger, but she had secretly poisoned it.

Aegeus recognizes Theseus

When Aegeus saw Theseus' sword and sandals he knew at once who he was, and moved to embrace him. As he did so he dropped the cup of wine. The contents fell on a dog at the king's feet, and killed it instantly. Aegeus then knew that Medea had tried to poison his son. She fled from Athens and never returned.

Theseus and the Minotaur

Some time after Theseus arrived in Athens, the Athenians became very unhappy. When Theseus asked why, he was told that once a year the Athenians had to send men and women to Crete, as food for a monster known as the **Minotaur**. It was half man, half bull, and had been born to the wife of **Minos**, the king of Crete. It lived in a maze known as the Labyrinth, which was so confusing that no one had ever found a way out. The Minotaur ate people who were thrown into the maze.

The voyage to Crete

Theseus volunteered to join the victims in order to kill the monster. Aegeus tried to persuade his son not to go, but Theseus boarded the ship, which had black sails. He promised that if he succeeded, he would change the sails to white ones on the return journey, so that Aegeus would know the outcome as soon as possible.

Into the Labyrinth

When Theseus got to Crete, Minos' daughter **Ariadne** fell in love with him. She gave him a sword to kill the Minotaur, and a ball of thread. Theseus tied one end of the thread to the entrance of the Labyrinth, and went inside. He found and killed the Minotaur, then followed the thread back outside. Ariadne, Theseus and his friends then fled from Crete.

Ariadne is abandoned

On the way back to Athens, they visited the island of Naxos. By this time Theseus was growing bored of Ariadne. While she was asleep, he called his friends back to the ship. They set sail, abandoning her. The gods disapproved, and punished Theseus by making him forget to hoist the white sails. Aegeus, watching from the shore for the ship, saw the black sails and thought that his son was dead. In his grief he threw himself off a cliff. Ever since, the sea where he died has been called the Aegean.

Theseus travels again

When Theseus heard about his father he was grief-stricken. To forget his sadness, he began to travel again. He went to the land of the **Amazons**, a tribe of warrior women, and married their queen. They returned to Athens, where a son, **Hippolytus**, was born. But the Amazon queen died soon afterwards.

Phaedra

Theseus married again. His new wife, Phaedra, was jealous of Hippolytus, and wanted to get rid of him. She told Theseus that Hippolytus had attacked her. The king was very angry, and asked **Poseidon** to punish his son. As Hippolytus was riding on the beach, Poseidon sent a huge wave to scare his horses. The horses bolted and Hippolytus was killed.

The death of Theseus

Phaedra was overcome with remorse. She confessed that she had lied, and then hanged herself. Theseus grew bitter after all these misfortunes, and became a very stern ruler. The Athenians turned against him and banished him. But after his death, Theseus' bones were returned to Athens, where a temple was built to him.

Oedipus

Oedipus was the son of **Laius** and **Jocasta**, the king and queen of Thebes in Boeotia. When he was born, they asked the priests of Apollo to foretell the child's fate. They were horrified to be told that Oedipus was destined to murder his father and marry his mother. To prevent this, Laius ordered one of his servants to take Oedipus away and kill him. The servant did not murder the child, but left him on a hillside to die. A shepherd found the baby and took him to Corinth, where the king and queen adopted him.

Oedipus consults the Oracle

When he grew up, Oedipus went to Delphi to consult the Oracle. He too was told that he would kill his father and marry his mother. Thinking the king and queen of Corinth were his parents, he left Corinth forever.

Oedipus' journey

On his travels, he came to a crossroads, where he saw a man being driven in a chariot. The driver called to him to make way, but Oedipus was used to being treated as a prince, and would not take orders. A fight began, and Oedipus killed the driver, the man and his servants. He did not know it, but the man was Laius. The first part of the prophecy had come true.

Oedipus and the Sphinx

As Oedipus continued on to Thebes, he met the **Sphinx**. She was a monster who sat by the city gates, and would asked a riddle of everyone who passed. When they couldn't answer, she ate them.

The Sphinx's riddle

Oedipus approached the Sphinx, and she asked him: What has four legs in the morning, two at midday, and three in the evening?

Oedipus realized the answer was a human being, who crawls, then walks, then, when old, uses a stick for support. The Sphinx was so angry at being defeated that she killed herself. The happy Thebans made Oedipus their king, and he married the queen, Jocasta.

The plague

All went well for some years, but then Thebes was hit by a plague. Many died, and the people turned to Oedipus to help them again. He sent messengers to consult the Oracle at Delphi, who declared that the plague would only end when Laius' murderer was found and punished.

Oedipus learns the truth

Messengers were sent to find out who had committed the murder. They discovered that it had been Oedipus. The servant who had taken the baby to the hillside confessed that he had not killed the child. Inquiries in Corinth confirmed that the baby had been adopted there. Oedipus realized that, without knowing it, he had murdered his father and married his mother. When she discovered what had happened, Jocasta killed herself. Oedipus blinded himself with her brooch, fled from Thebes and died, ruined, at Colonnus near Athens.

The curse of the family of Atreus

Atreus became king of Mycenae when he married **Aerope**, a Mycenaean princess. But legend records that Atreus was under several curses, which caused him and his family great suffering and misery.

Tantalus offends the gods

Atreus' grandfather **Tantalus** had been a friend of **Zeus**, and was allowed to eat with the gods. But he stole their food and gave it to his friends. Then he asked the gods to a banquet, and tested them to see if they truly were all-powerful. He killed his son **Pelops** and served him at the feast, though it was forbidden to eat human flesh. The gods knew at once what had happened. Zeus condemned Tantalus to eternal torment in the Underworld, and put a curse on his family.

Pelops returns from the dead

Zeus brought Pelops back to life. When the boy grew up he fell in love with a princess, **Hippodamia**. Her father, King **Oenomaus**, had been told by fortune tellers that he would be killed by his son-in-law, and so wished to stop anyone from marrying his daughter. He challenged her suitors to a chariot race, stating that the loser would be executed. The god **Poseidon** lent Pelops some of his horses. Pelops also bribed the king's charioteer **Myrtilus,** offering him a reward if he sabotaged the king's chariot.

The chariot race

Oenomaus was killed in a crash during the chariot race, and Pelops escaped with Hippodamia and Myrtilus. But, instead of rewarding the charioteer, Pelops murdered him, to keep the sabotage plot quiet. As he was dying, Myrtilus placed a curse on Pelops.

A third curse

Later, Atreus himself was the victim of a curse. He found out that his wife had been seduced by his brother **Thyestes**. He took his revenge by killing all of his brother's sons except one. Thyestes then put a curse on his brother.

The curses are fulfilled

The curses were eventually fulfilled during the reign of **Agamemnon**, Atreus' son. **Menelaus**, Agamemnon's brother had married **Helen**, the queen of Sparta. Helen was so beautiful that all the Greek kings had fallen in love with her. But, realizing Helen's beauty could cause conflict between them, they had all taken an oath that they would help the man she married, if anyone tried to steal her away. Unfortunately, the goddess of love, **Aphrodite**, had promised Helen to a Trojan prince named **Paris**. He went to Sparta and Helen soon fell in love with him. They ran away together to Troy.

Agamemnon plots his revenge

Agamemnon was very angry about Helen's treatment of Menelaus. He reminded the other Greek kings of their oath and organized an expedition to Troy to bring Helen back. To ensure the troops had good winds for the sea journey he even killed his daughter **Iphigenia** as a sacrifice to the gods. The war against Troy lasted ten years, with many deaths on both sides, before the Greeks won and Agamemnon returned home.

Agamemnon is murdered

Meanwhile, Agamemnon's wife **Clytemnestra** was furious about the sacrifice of her daughter Iphigenia, and about her husband's long absence. She fell in love with **Aegistus**, her husband's cousin and enemy, and married him. She pretended to welcome Agamemnon when he came home, but then murdered him. She and Aegistus then ruled Mycenae.

Revenge and the end of the curse

Agamemnon's son **Orestes** found out that his mother had killed his father and took his revenge by murdering Clytemnestra and Aegistus. By killing his own mother, Orestes had committed a terrible crime. He was driven mad by the **Furies**, goddesses with dogs' heads and bats' wings who tormented murderers. Finally the gods intervened, as they decided that Orestes had suffered enough. They cleansed Orestes of his guilt, and ended the curse. Orestes became king of Mycenae.

Two poems by Homer

The earliest surviving examples of Greek literature are two epic poems, the *Iliad* and the *Odyssey*. They are thought to be by a poet named Homer, who passed his poems on by word of mouth. The poems were so popular that, when writing became widespread in Greece, later scholars and poets wrote them down. The *Iliad* and the *Odyssey* have inspired generations of readers, writers and historians, and provide us with a wealth of information about the early Greek world.

The *Iliad*

The *Iliad* takes place during the last few weeks of the Trojan War. It concerns an argument between the hero **Achilles** and the leader of the Greek forces, **Agamemnon**. Agamemnon stole a slave-girl from Achilles, who was insulted and withdrew from the fighting. Without him, the Greeks were downhearted and suffered terrible losses. To boost the troops' morale, Achilles' friend **Patroclus** dressed like Achilles and went into battle. Thinking he was Achilles, a Trojan warrior called **Hector** killed him.

Achilles, full of remorse, returned to the battlefield and killed Hector. He dragged the body around the walls of Troy behind a chariot. Hector's father, **Priam**, paid a ransom to Achilles, who finally returned the body. Hector was given a hero's funeral.

The poem contains many episodes about other heroes and their deeds. The human events are mirrored by episodes about the gods and goddesses, who each take sides in the dispute.

The *Odyssey*

The *Odyssey* tells the story of another hero **Odysseus**, who was clever and cunning, and suggested the trick of the wooden horse. After the Trojan War, Odysseus tried to return home to Ithaca, where his wife **Penelope** was being pestered by suitors. They thought Odysseus was dead, and wanted to marry her for her wealth. They insisted that she choose one of them as a husband.

Much of the *Odyssey* tells of Odysseus' journey home, and of the many dangers he encountered. He had to kill the one-eyed monster, **Cyclops**, and survive many shipwrecks. He also escaped from the **Sirens**, creatures whose singing lured ships to crash on to the rocks, and from **Circe**, a witch who turned men into animals.

When he reached Ithaca, the goddess **Athene** disguised him as a beggar, to help him return to his house unnoticed. To buy time, Penelope had organized an impossibly hard archery competition for her suitors, saying she would marry the winner. Odysseus, still disguised, took part in the competition and won. He then killed the other competitors. Finally Penelope recognized him and they were reunited.

Who was who in ancient Greece

Below is a list of the important people mentioned in this book, with details of their lives. If a person's name appears in **bold type** in the text of an entry, then that person also has his or her own entry in this list.

Aeschylus (c.525-455BC) Writer of tragic plays. He wrote around 90 plays, but only seven survive. Most of his tragedies were stories of the gods and heroes. His most famous work is the *Oresteia*, a group of three plays about King Agamemnon and his family. Aeschylus is regarded as the founder of Greek tragedy. He was the first writer to use more than one actor, introducing dialogue and action on stage.

Alcibiades (c.450-404BC) Athenian politician. He was a pupil of **Socrates** and the ward of **Pericles**, who was a close relative. In 420BC he was elected *strategos*. During the Peloponnesian War, he persuaded the Athenians to send troops to Sicily and was appointed one of the leaders of the expedition. But he was recalled, to face the charge that he had defaced statues in Athens with a group of his aristocratic friends. Instead he fled to Sparta, where he advised the Spartans how to fight their war against Athens. In 407BC he was recalled to Athens and reelected. But he was held responsible for the Athenian defeat at the Battle of Notium, and retired. He was assassinated in Persia.

Alexander the Great (356-323BC) Macedonian king and military leader. A pupil of **Aristotle**, he learned military tactics as a soldier in the army of his father, **Philip II of Macedonia**. In 336BC, Philip was murdered, and Alexander became king at the age of 20. He was a military genius, and, after taking control of Greece and areas to the north, he invaded Asia. Eventually he conquered the largest empire in the ancient world. Alexander married a Persian princess named Roxane. He died of a fever at Babylon, aged 32.

Anaxagoras (c.500-c.428BC) Philosopher. He wrote *On Nature*, a book which influenced many later philosophers. Anaxagoras deduced that the Sun was a mass of flaming material and that the Moon reflected its light. He was also the first to explain a solar eclipse.

Antigonas II (c.320-239BC) Macedonian king. He ruled from 279BC to 239BC. As king of Macedonia he also ruled Greece itself, and was one of the most powerful leaders of the Hellenistic World. His successors ruled until 146BC, when Macedonia and Greece were eventually conquered by the Romans.

Archimedes (c.287-212BC) Mathematician, astronomer and inventor. He studied at the Museum in Alexandria and then lived in Syracuse. He invented a type of pulley and a device for raising water. He also discovered an important law of physics – that an object displaces its own volume of water.

Aristides (c.520-467BC) Athenian politician and general. He came from an aristocratic family. Aristides was a prominent leader at the time of the Persian Wars and was a *strategos* at the Battle of Marathon. He was ostracized in 482BC, but was recalled a year later and took part in the battles of Salamis and Plataea. Aristides also helped to set up the Delian League.

Aristophanes (5th century BC-c.385BC) Athenian writer of comic plays. He wrote around 40 comedies, of which eleven survive. Some of these make fun of the political events of the time. Many of his works won prizes at the Athens Drama Festival. His most famous plays are *The Wasps*, *The Birds* and *The Frogs*.

Aristotle (384-322BC) Athenian philosopher. He studied with **Plato** in Athens, then visited the eastern Mediterranean. After spending three years as the tutor of **Alexander the Great**, he returned to Athens in 335BC. He set up a school, the Lyceum, but after Alexander's death he was charged with impiety and fled to Euboea. His writings cover many subjects, such as poetry, political life, and various philosophical theories. His famous works include *Poetics*, *Politics* and *Metaphysics*.

Aspasia (born c.465BC) Wife of **Pericles**. She came from Miletus, and was never properly accepted by many Athenians. She was often mocked by Pericles' enemies, and by comedy writers. But she was very beautiful and well-educated, and **Socrates** and his friends thought highly her. In 431BC she was prosecuted, but acquitted.

Cimon (late 6th century BC-c.450BC) Athenian soldier and statesman. He was the son of **Miltiades**, and a sworn enemy of the Persians. After the Greek victory over the Persians at the battles of Salamis and Plataea, Cimon led expeditions to free the Greek islands from Persian rule. He was responsible for several later victories against the Persians. In 462BC he persuaded Athens to support Sparta. When the Spartans refused Athenian help Cimon's prestige suffered and he was ostracized in 461BC. He was later recalled, and negotiated the 5-year peace with Sparta. He led an expedition to Cyprus, where he died.

Cleisthenes (lived 6th century BC) Athenian politician. He was a member of the Athenian aristocracy, and took power in Athens after the overthrow of the tyrant Hippias. In 580BC he introduced reforms that led to the political system known as democracy. He also introduced the system of ostracism to the city.

Draco (lived 7th century BC) Athenian politician. In 621BC he was appointed to improve the Athenian legal system. He encouraged public trials so people could see that justice had been done. He made existing Athenian laws much more severe, and introduced the death penalty for many minor crimes. The Athenians became unhappy with such severe laws, and the system was later reformed again by **Solon**.

Euclid (lived c.300BC) Mathematician. He worked in Alexandria, and wrote several books about mathematics and geometry. His best known book was *Elements*, part of which sums up the teachings of mathematicians who worked before him. Several of his theories and discoveries remain in use today.

Euripides (c.485-406BC) Athenian writer of tragic plays. He wrote over 90 plays. We know the titles of 80, but only 19 of them have survived to the present day. Among his best known plays are *Medea*, *The Trojan Women* and *Orestes*. He won a total of five first prizes at the Athens Drama Festival. Later he moved to the court of King Archelaus of Macedonia, where he eventually died.

Herodotus (c.484-420BC) Historian. Herodotus was born in Halicarnassus in Ionia. He visited Egypt, the Black Sea, Babylon and Cyrene, then lived on Samos. Later he moved to Athens, but he finally settled in Thurii in southern Italy. Herodotus is known as 'the Father of History'. He wrote a history of the Greek people based around the Persian Wars. It also included information on many other subjects. Herodotus was one of the first writers to interview eyewitnesses, to compare historical facts and to see them as a sequence of linked events. But his accounts are not always reliable.

Hesiod (lived c.8th century BC) Boeotian poet. He owned a farm at Ascra in Boeotia. He claimed that the Muses came to visit him one day on Mount Helicon and gave him the gift of poetry. His best known book is *Works and Days*, which includes practical details of farming, a calendar of lucky and unlucky days, and an explanation of religious ceremonies. He is also thought to have written *The Theogony*, an account of the Greek gods and goddesses and their relationships.

Hippocrates (c.460-c.377BC) Doctor and writer on medicine. His teachings became the basis of medical ideas throughout the ancient world. Unlike many earlier Greek doctors, he based his work on close observations of his patients, rather than on religious rituals. His writings discuss many aspects of medicine, including the way a doctor should behave, and the effect of the environment on disease and illness. Hippocrates lived on the island of Kos, where he founded an important medical school.

Homer (lived c.9th century BC) Poet. Very little is known about Homer. He is thought to have been a bard who recited his poetry. For many years, the poems thought to have been composed by Homer were passed on by word of mouth. Eventually, centuries later, fragments were written down by other poets and historians. According to tradition, Homer came from the island of Chios, and he may have been blind. The poems thought to be by Homer, *The Iliad* and *The Odyssey*, are detailed accounts of events during and after the Trojan War.

Miltiades (c.550-489BC) Athenian soldier and politician, father of **Cimon**. He was sent by the tyrant Hippias to the Chersonese to make sure that the Athenians kept control of the route to the Black Sea. Later he fought for the Persians, but joined the Ionian revolt in 500BC. When the revolt was defeated he had to flee to Athens. He led the Athenian forces at the Battle of Marathon, which the Greeks won, largely thanks to Miltiades' superior military skills. Later he led the Athenians in an unsuccessful expedition to Paros. He returned to Athens, where he was tried and fined a huge sum of money.

Myron (lived 5th century BC) Sculptor. He worked in Athens between around 460 and 440BC. His most famous statues included one of the runner Ladas, and one of a man throwing a discus.

Peisistratus (c.590-527BC) Athenian politician. In 546BC, after two earlier attempts to seize power, he declared himself tyrant of Athens. Under his rule Athens prospered. He reorganized public finances, and spent public money on roads and a good water supply. He also rebuilt and improved much of Athens, and encouraged art and literature. Athenian trade with the rest of Greece also improved because Peisistratus was an excellent diplomat and wanted good relations with other areas. He died while still in power.

Pericles (early 5th century BC-429BC) Athenian statesman and general. He became the most powerful politician of his day. He was elected *strategos* every year from 443BC to 429BC, and was such a powerful speaker that he could usually swing public opinion his way. He refined the Athenian democratic system, arranged for the rebuilding of the Acropolis and the construction of the Long Walls. In 430BC he was charged with stealing public funds and fined a huge sum of money. He was still elected *strategos* the following year, but died in the plague that hit Athens.

Pheidias (c.500-c.425BC) Athenian sculptor. He mostly used bronze, but was best known for his cult statues in ivory and gold. He made the frieze around the Parthenon and the statue of Athene there, as well as the statue of Zeus at Olympus. He was accused of taking the gold given to him for decorations on the Parthenon, but escaped and went to work at Olympus. Later he was again charged with fraud, and died in prison.

Philip II of Macedonia (c.382-336BC) Macedonian king and military leader. He began ruling Macedonia in 359BC. He reorganized the army, and showed great skill as a military commander and diplomat. Philip united the country, extended the frontiers and made Macedonia into the greatest military power of its day. He married a princess called Olympias, and they had a son, **Alexander**. He was assassinated in 336BC, possibly by poison. Some historians think his wife and son may have been involved in the murder plot.

Pindar (c.518-438BC) Athenian poet. He was born in Boeotia, and went to Athens at an early age. He was a friend of **Aeschylus**, and quickly became known as a poet. Ancient scholars divided his many poems into 17 books according to themes and styles. Some poems celebrating winners at games, some addressed to tyrants, and a few other fragments have survived. Many later writers described him as the greatest Greek poet.

Plato (c.429-347BC) Athenian philosopher. He was a member of an aristocratic Athenian family, and a pupil of **Socrates**. After Socrates died, Plato fled to Megara, then lived in Syracuse. Later he returned to Athens, where he wrote *The Apology*, an answer to Socrates' enemies. His ideas for running an ideal state were set out in his books *The Republic* and *The Laws*. He founded a school on the outskirts of Athens, in a grove known as the Academy, which gave the school its name. The school was famous throughout the ancient world, and continued for centuries after Plato's death. It was closed in AD529 by the Roman emperor Justinian, who thought it was politically dangerous. Plato's ideas have remained influential to the present day.

Praxiteles (born c.390BC) Athenian sculptor. Little is known about his life, except that he worked in Athens. His sculpture of the goddess Aphrodite (see page 47) is the first known statue of the female nude. Praxiteles also made beautiful sculptures of the gods Hermes, Eros and Apollo.

Ptolemy I (305-284BC) Macedonian general, later King of Egypt. He took over as ruler of Egypt after the death of **Alexander the Great** in 323BC. He and his successors ruled successfully until Egypt was eventually conquered by the Romans in 30BC.

Pythagoras (c.580BC-late 6th century BC) Philosopher and mathematician. He may have spent some time in Egypt and the East. Later he founded a school at Croton in southern Italy. Nothing has survived of his writings, but we know about his teachings from contemporary descriptions. He thought that after people died their souls lived on in other beings. He also developed many geometrical and mathematical theories.

Sappho (born c.612BC) Poet. Sappho was born on the island of Lesbos, but probably left there to travel to Sicily. For a time she ran a school for girls. It is thought that she wrote nine books of poetry, but only a few fragments of her poems survive. Sappho was considered one of the greatest Greek poets. She died in the middle of the 6th century BC.

Seleucus I (died 280BC) Macedonian general, later Middle Eastern king. In 304BC he seized a vast area of the empire of **Alexander the Great**, and became one of the three main rulers of the Hellenistic World. But the empire was too big to hold together and it was eventually conquered by the Romans in 64BC.

Socrates (c.469-399BC) Athenian philosopher. He never wrote his ideas down, but discussed points of philosophy with his pupils. Socrates and his pupils pointed out weak points in the government, and in people's beliefs. This made them unpopular with politicians. Eventually his enemies charged him with disrespecting the religion and corrupting the young. He was sentenced to death by drinking poison. We know about Socrates' ideas because they were written down by his pupils, including **Plato**.

Solon (c.640-558BC) Athenian politician. He became *archon* in around 594BC, and quickly passed many new laws. These included bringing debtors back from exile, and the cancellation of many debts. He set up a new court to which people could appeal if they thought they had been wrongly tried, and also reformed the way the government took decisions. Solon encouraged craftsmen from other parts of Greece to come to Athens, and granted them citizenship. By making Athenians use the same money as other Greek states he also encouraged trade and industry.

Sophocles (c.496-405BC) Athenian writer of tragic plays. Of his 123 plays, only seven survive. The best known are *Antigone*, *Oedipus Tyrannus* and *Electra*. Sophocles was among the first to write plays with more than two characters, and one of the first to use stage scenery. Before him, plays concentrated on myths and the affairs of the gods. Although his plays were still about myths, they were seen from the human viewpoint.

Themistocles (c.524-459BC) Athenian statesman. He was *strategos* at the Battle of Marathon (see page 40) and persuaded the Athenians to build up their navy. In 480-479BC he organized resistance to the Persians. His strategy helped the Athenians to win the Battle of Salamis. Later he organized the rebuilding of the walls of Athens in 479-478BC. Around 471BC he was ostracized and fled to Argos. He was accused of treason. Then he fled to Asia Minor where the Persians, grateful to him for his part in negotiating peace with Athens, made him governor of three cities.

Thucydides (c.460-396BC) Athenian historian. In 424BC he was elected *strategos* but was held responsible for a military defeat and was ostracized. He did not return to Athens for 20 years. Thucydides wrote an account of the Peloponnesian War which is considered to be one of the first history books. As well as describing the war itself, it gives many valuable details about life in Athens and elsewhere.

Xenophon (c.430-354BC) Athenian historian. He was a pupil of **Socrates**. He fought as a mercenary soldier for both the Persians and the Spartans, and was banished from Athens as a result. While in exile in Sparta he wrote many books, including *The Anabasis*, about his period with the Persians, and *The Hellenica*, a history of the events of his day. He also wrote about farming, horses and riding, finance and about Socrates.

Date chart

This chart lists the most important dates in ancient Greek history. It also includes some of the events that took place elsewhere in the world during the same period. These are shown in *italic type*.

Early history

from 40,000BC The first people settle in Greece.

The Neolithic Period: c.6500-2900BC

c.6500-3000BC First inhabitants settle on Crete and introduce farming. Pottery is made in Greece and Crete.

c.6250BC Çatal Hüyük in Anatolia (modern Turkey) becomes the largest town of its time. Pottery and wool cloth are manufactured there.

c.5000-4000BC Farming spreads through Europe.

c.4000BC Evidence of early inhabitants in the Cyclades islands, including remains of metalware.

c.3500BC The wheel is invented in the Middle East.

c.3200BC Pottery introduced in Ecuador, South America.

c.3100BC Cities develop in Sumer. Writing develops in Sumer and Egypt.

The Bronze Age: c.2900-1000BC

c.2900BC Metal is now in widespread use. The population of Greece increases, some villages grow into towns and some people become specialized craft workers. Trade flourishes.

c.2686-2181BC Old Kingdom in Egypt

c.2590BC Pyramid of Cheops is built in Giza in Egypt.

c.2500BC The city of Troy is founded.

c.2500BC Beginning of Indus civilization in India.

c.2100BC Possible arrival of the first Greek-speaking people in Greece.

c.2000BC The sail is first used on ships in the Aegean.

c.2000BC Building of Stonehenge begins in Britain.

c.2000BC Middle Kingdom begins in Egypt.

c.1814BC First Assyrian Empire begins in the Middle East.

c.1900BC The first Cretan palaces are built. Rise of Minoan culture on Crete.

c.1700BC The Cretan palaces are destroyed by earthquakes, then rebuilt.

c.1600BC Rise of Mycenaean culture in Greece. The first shaft graves are built.

c.1600BC Towns and cities develop in China.

c.1567BC New Kingdom begins in Egypt.

c.1550BC Aryans settle in northern India and establish the Hindu religion.

c.1500BC Writing in use in China.

c.1500BC Tholos tombs are first used in Greece.

c.1500-1450BC Traditional date for eruption of Thera.

c.1450BC Cretan palaces are destroyed. The palace at Knossos is taken over by Mycenaeans and rebuilt.

c.1400BC Knossos burns down, and is not rebuilt.

c.1250BC Strong walls are built at Mycenae and other mainland sites. Date traditionally given for the start of the Trojan War.

c.1200BC Mycenaean power declines and many of their cities are abandoned. Migration of the Sea Peoples begins.

c.1200BC Jewish religion begins.

c.1166BC Death of Ramesses III, last Egyptian Pharaoh.

c.1150BC Olmec civilization begins in Mexico.

The Dark Ages: c.1100-800BC

by 1100BC The Mycenaean way of life has broken down.

c.1100BC Phoenicians spread throughout the Mediterranean, and develop alphabetic writing.

c.1000BC Etruscans arrive in Italy.

c.911BC New Assyrian Empire begins.

c.900BC The state of Sparta is founded.

814BC Phoenicians found city of Carthage on the North African coast.

The Archaic Period: c.800-500BC

Between 850-750BC Homer probably lived at this time.

c.800BC Greek contact with the other peoples of the Mediterranean resumes. The Greeks adopt the Phoenician style of writing, using it for their own language.

c.800BC Aryan people move southward in India.

776BC First Olympic Games held.

753BC Date traditionally given for the founding of Rome.

c.750-650BC Groups of people start to emigrate from Greece. They found colonies around the Mediterranean.

c.740-720BC The Spartans begin expanding their territory, and conquer the state of Messenia.

c.650BC The first tyrants seize power in Greek mainland states. First coins used in Lydia.

c.650BC Iron Age begins in China.

c.630-613BC The Messenians revolt against the Spartans but are eventually crushed.

621BC Draco is appointed *archon* in Athens and introduces a strict set of laws.

c.594BC Solon begins to reform Athens' political system.

c.550BC Tyrannies are established in the Greek colonies.

c.546BC Peisistratus seizes power as tyrant of Athens.

c.530BC Beginning of the Persian Wars

by 521BC *King Darius I has expanded the Persian Empire from the Nile river to the Indus river.*

513BC The Persians invade Europe.

c.510BC *Monarchy in Rome is replaced by a republic.*

508BC Cleisthenes seizes power in Athens and introduces reforms which lead to democracy.

500-499BC The Greek colonies in Ionia revolt against Persian rule.

The Classical Age: c.500-336BC

494BC The Persians suppress the Ionian revolt.

490BC The Persians defeated at the Battle of Marathon.

480BC Battles of Thermopylae and Salamis.

479BC Battle of Plataea. Persians are repelled from Greece.

479BC *Death of the Chinese religious teacher Confucius.*

478BC Athens and other Greek states form the Delian League against the Persians.

460-457BC The Long Walls are built around Athens and Piraeus. The Acropolis is rebuilt.

c.450BC *Start of Celtic culture known as La Tène, named after the site in France where evidence of it was first found.*

449BC The Delian League makes peace with Persia.

445BC 30 Years' Peace treaty between Athens and Sparta.

443-429BC Pericles elected *strategos* every year.

431-404BC Peloponnesian War between Athens and Sparta.

421BC 50 Years' Peace treaty between Sparta and Athens.

413BC War breaks out again between Athens and Sparta.

407BC Athenian fleet defeated at Notium.

405BC Athens defeated by Sparta at Battle of Aegospotami.

404BC Sparta defeats Athens in Peloponnesian War. Athens forced to adopt rule of oligarchs, the Thirty Tyrants.

403BC Democracy is reinstated in Athens.

399BC Wars between Sparta and Persia begin.

395-387BC The Corinthian War. Alliance of Corinth, Athens, Argos and Thebes against Sparta.

394BC The Persians defeat Sparta at the Battle of Cnidus.

387BC Corinthian War ended by King's Peace, negotiated by the Persians. Ionian colonies pass to Persian control.

371BC The Thebans defeat Sparta at the Battle of Leuctra.

362BC Sparta and Athens defeat Thebes at the Battle of Mantinea.

359BC Philip II becomes king of Macedonia.

340BC Greek states form the Hellenic League against Philip.

338BC Philip defeats the Hellenic League at the Battle of Chaeronea, and becomes ruler of Greece.

337BC All Greek states except Sparta form the Corinthian league, led by Philip. The league declares war on Persia.

336BC Philip dies and is succeeded by his son Alexander.

332BC Alexander conquers Phoenicia, Samaria, Judaea, Gaza and Egypt.

331BC Sparta joins the Corinthian League. Alexander defeats the Persians at the Battle of Gaugamela.

327BC Alexander conquers Persia, and advances into India.

323BC Alexander dies in Babylon.

The Hellenistic Period: c.323-30BC

323-322BC The Lamian Wars. The Greek states fight to win independence from the Macedonians, but are defeated.

323-281BC Wars of the *Diadochi* (Alexander's successors).

301BC Battle of Ipsus. Four rival diadochi kingdoms set up.

281BC Battle of Corupedium ends the Wars of the Diadochi. Three diadochi kingdoms established: Macedonia, Asia Minor and Egypt.

275BC *Rome defeats King Pyrrhus of Epirus in Italy.*

266-262BC The Chremonides War. The Athenians rise against the Antigonids but are suppressed.

221-179BC Reign of Philip V of Macedonia

215BC Philip V forms an alliance with Hannibal of Carthage, provoking Roman reprisals.

215-205BC First Macedonian Wars between Macedonia and Rome.

202-197BC Second Macedonian War. Philip V is defeated by the Romans and gives up control of Greece.

179-168BC Reign of last Macedonian king, Perseus.

171-168BC Third Macedonian War. Romans defeat Perseus at the Battle of Pydna. They abolish the Macedonian monarchy and set up four Roman republics.

147-146BC The Achaean War. The Romans impose direct Roman rule on Greece and Macedonia.

Glossary

This glossary is a list of the ancient Greek words used in this book, as well as some English words that may be unfamiliar. Usually, the term given in **bold type** is the singular, with the plural in brackets, such as **amphora** (amphorae).

Acropolis A fortified city, built on high ground. In Mycenaean times it contained much of the city. Later it was used as a religious sanctuary as part of a larger city.

agora An open space, in the middle of a Greek city, used for markets and as a meeting place.

amphora (amphorae) A large pot with two handles, used to transport and store wine and other liquids.

andron A dining room in a private house, used by men.

archon An Athenian official. *Archons* were very powerful in the Archaic Period, but were less important when democracy was introduced.

aristocrat A member of a rich, landowning family.

Attica The name of the state made up of Athens and the surrounding countryside.

barbarian Any foreigner who did not speak Greek. It came to mean any uncivilized people.

black figure ware A style of pottery decorated with black figures on a red background.

Bronze Age The time from c.3000-1100BC when bronze was the main metal used for making weapons and other tools.

caryatid A column carved in the shape of a woman.

cella The main room of a temple, where the statue of a god or goddess stood.

chiton A woman's dress made from one piece of cloth.

chorus A group of men who took part in plays. They all spoke together, often commenting on the action. Sometimes they also sang and danced.

citizen A free man who had the right to participate in the government of his city-state.

Corinthian column A style of column whith carved acanthus leaves at its top.

cuirass Body protection used by hoplite soldiers, consisting of a breastplate and backplate joined by straps.

cult statue A statue of the god or goddess which stood in the main room of a temple.

democracy A political system in which all citizens had a say in the government of their state. The word comes from the Greek for 'rule by the people'.

Diadochi The name given to the generals who took over the various parts of Alexander the Great's empire after his death. The word means 'successors'.

Doric column A plain column with an undecorated top. The *Doric Order* was a style of architecture which used this sort of column.

electrum A natural mixture of gold and silver, which was used to make the first coins.

ephebe A young Athenian man engaged in two years' compulsory military training.

faience Glazed earthenware used in Minoan Crete to make decorative objects.

fresco A wall painting made by painting wet plaster.

greave A leg protector used by hoplite soldiers. It covered the front of the leg from knee to ankle.

gymnasium (gymnasia) A place where people could train in athletics. Later a gymnasium was often the focus of a city's intellectual life too, and might be equipped with a lecture hall and a library.

Hellene The word which the Greeks used to refer to the whole Greek race. It came from the name of a legendary hero Hellen, said to be the father of the Greek people.

Hellenistic Age A term used to describe the period after the death of Alexander the Great, when Greek language and culture dominated the countries of his former empire.

herm A statue of the god Hermes. It usually stood outside a house and was thought to protect the home.

hetaira (hetairai) A woman specially educated to make conversation and play music in order to entertain men.

himation A cloak or scarf, worn by men and women.

hoplite A heavily armed Greek foot soldier.

Ionic column A tall column, with two swirls, known as volutes, decorating the top. The *Ionic Order*, a style of architecture which used this sort of column, was popular in Greece's eastern colonies and islands.

krater A large pot in which wine was mixed with water, before being poured out.

labrys A double headed weapon, which was an important sacred symbol in Minoan religion.

libation An offering of liquid (wine, milk or blood), poured onto an altar or the earth in a religious ceremony.

Linear A An early form of writing used by the Minoans.

Linear B An adapted form of Linear A writing, used by the Mycenaeans.

Long Walls The walls which linked the city of Athens to its port at Piraeus from 460 to 404BC.

lyre A stringed musical instrument, made from a tortoise shell and ox horns. Later lyres were wooden.

megaron A hall in a Mycenaean palace, containing four pillars and a hearth, where kings conducted state business.

metic A foreign resident living in Athens.

Minoan The name the archaeologist, Arthur Evans, gave to the civilization he discovered on Crete. The term came from the legendary Cretan king Minos.

museum A temple to the Muses (see page 54). The most famous one was built in Alexandria in Egypt in the Hellenistic Age. Scientists and inventors worked there.

mystery cult A religion with rituals that were kept very secret. Only people who had been initiated into the religion could attend its ceremonies.

oligarchy A political system in which a small group of people governed.

omen A sign which warned of good or evil to come. Specially trained priests saw omens in the livers of sacrificed animals, or in the flight patterns of birds.

oracle The word can mean three things: a sacred place where people consulted a god or goddess; the priest or priestess who spoke on behalf of the deity; or the message from the deity. The most famous was at the Temple of Apollo in Delphi, where a priestess known as the Pythia was thought to be able to communicate with the gods.

ostracism A special vote held in the Athenian Assembly to banish unpopular politicians. It is so called because the voters scratched the names of people they wanted to expel onto *ostraka*, pieces of broken pottery.

paidagogos A special slave who escorted a boy to and from school and supervised him in class.

patron deity A god or goddess who was thought to protect a particular place, person or group of people.

peltast A lightly armed foot soldier, first used by the Thracians and later by the Greek armies.

peristyle A row of columns surrounding a temple.

phalanx The formation in which hoplite soldiers fought, consisting of a block of soldiers, usually eight ranks deep.

philosopher The first philosophers were scholars who studied all aspects of the world around them. Later philosophers began trying to understand the purpose of the universe and the nature of human life.

pithos (pithoi) A large storage jar used in Minoan Crete.

polis An independent Greek state, consisting of a city and the surrounding countryside.

Pythia The priestess who spoke on behalf of the god Apollo at the Oracle of Delphi.

red figure ware A style of pottery decorated with red figures on a black background.

relief A sculpture carved into a flat slab of stone.

rhapsode A poet who made his living by reciting poetry at religious festivals or private parties.

rhyton A pot shaped like a horn or an animal's head, with a hole in the lower end that acted as a spout.

sarcophagus A stone coffin.

shaft grave An early form of Mycenaean tomb, in which the body was buried in a pit at the bottom of a deep shaft.

soothsayer Someone who was thought to be able to foresee the future.

stele (stelae) A stone slab used to mark a grave.

stoa A long, roofed passageway with columns on one side which provided shelter from the sun, wind and rain. The *stoa* often formed the side of an *agora* and sometimes contained stalls or offices.

strategos (strategoi) An Athenian army commander. Ten *strategoi* were elected each year. Under the democratic system, *strategoi* also had the power to implement the policies decided by the Council and the Assembly.

terracotta A mixture of clay and sand baked to make tiles and small statues.

tholos A Mycenaean, beehive-shaped tomb at the end of a long corridor. Later the name was also given to circular buildings with conical roofs.

trireme A warship with three rows of oars.

tyrant A Greek word for 'ruler'. A tyrant was someone who governed with absolute power. Later the word came to mean any cruel, oppressive ruler.

Index

Page numbers in *italic type* indicate map references.